LIBRARY TECHNOLOGY BUYING STRATEGIES

For Reference
Not to be taken from this room

LIBRARY TECHNOLOGY BUYING STRATEGIES

EDITED BY
MARSHALL BREEDING

An imprint of the American Library Association

CHICAGO   2016

MARSHALL BREEDING is an independent consultant, speaker, and author. He is the creator and editor of the Library Technology Guides website, editor of *Smart Libraries Newsletter* and a columnist for *Computers in Libraries*. He has authored the annual "Automation Marketplace" feature published most recently in *American Libraries*. He has also edited or authored several books, including *Cloud Computing for Libraries*. Formerly the director for innovative technology and research for the Vanderbilt University Library, he regularly teaches workshops and gives presentations internationally at library conferences.

© 2016 by the American Library Association

Extensive effort has gone into ensuring the reliability of the information in this book; however, the publisher makes no warranty, express or implied, with respect to the material contained herein.

ISBN: 978-0-8389-1467-0 (paper)

Library of Congress Cataloging-in-Publication Data
Names: Breeding, Marshall, editor.
Title: Library technology buying strategies / edited by Marshall Breeding.
Description: Chicago : ALA Editions, an imprint of the American Library Association, 2016. | Includes bibliographical references and index.
Identifiers: LCCN 2016013269 | ISBN 9780838914670 (print : alk. paper)
Subjects: LCSH: Libraries—Information technology—Purchasing. | Integrated library systems (Computer systems)—Purchasing. | Libraries—Automation—Contracting out. | Computer systems—Purchasing. | Library information networks. | Electronic information resources—Management.
Classification: LCC Z678.9 .L5185 2016 | DDC 025.00285—dc23
LC record available at https://lccn.loc.gov/2016013269

Cover design by Alejandra Diaz. Cover imagery © Shutterstock, Inc.

Text composition by Dianne M. Rooney in the Chaparral, Gotham, and Bell Gothic typefaces.

♾ This paper meets the requirements of ANSI/NISO Z39.48-1992 (Permanence of Paper).

Printed in the United States of America

20 19 18 17 16   5 4 3 2 1

Contents

Preface

I have devoted most of my professional energy throughout my career to technologies that support the work of libraries. I am delighted to pass along some practical advice in this *Library Technology Buyer's Guide*.

The prospect of moving to a new automation system can be daunting. When do the benefits of moving to something new surpass the deficits of keeping the incumbent? Can the products on the market deliver what libraries need to survive and prosper? Are those based on open source more flexible than the proprietary systems? What about those deployed in the cloud? These and dozens more questions arise as libraries enter a selection process. In consultation with Patrick Hogan, senior editor for ALA TechSource, I edited this volume and wrote several of its newly updated chapters to offer guidance in finding answers to these questions and in providing the background and perspective among the many options available today.

I have been intensely involved with library automation systems for more than thirty years. It has been interesting to see these systems progress from the mainframes era, through the phase of client/server systems, and more recently into web-based platforms. My perspective has been informed through my twenty-seven-year career working with technology from hands-on to administrative and strategic levels at Vanderbilt University Library, through opportunities to work with dozens of libraries of all kinds as a consultant, and through countless writing and research projects. These experiences have given me information and perspective across the spectrum of topics in library technology which can potentially benefit others in the field as they evaluate and eventually purchase new systems.

Acquiring an automation system has never been more complex; new categories of products have emerged that may or may not be a good fit for any given library. Resource management and discovery may be implemented together or separately. Products from several different vendors or created through open source projects populate each category. This volume was assembled to guide libraries in identifying the best technical infrastructure, whether in the form of a single comprehensive product or multiple components. Even though the number of choices has narrowed, libraries face tough choices among product categories and competitive options. It is important to face any evaluation process armed with independent information to balance the content provided by organizations as they promote their products.

My aim is to provide substance beyond the buzzwords and hype. Chapters will outline some of the major trends seen in the library technology field. Some themes covered include the new genre of library services platforms, the ongoing advancement of integrated library systems, the role of discovery services, and basic technology trends such as cloud computing.

The content especially benefits anyone in a library facing an immediate or upcoming process to select a new automation system or discovery environment. Administrators or managers who don't necessarily come with a deep technological background will learn about the types of technology products available and what functionality might best suit their organization. The book will help new systems librarians or other practitioners who need to rapidly acquire practical information related to tech products and the vendor community. More experienced technologists can update their awareness of the current offerings and may benefit from the procedural overview of the RFP (request for proposal) process. Students of library and information will likely face the prospect of reviewing or changing systems at some point during their career, and this volume can add an element to their education to help them adeptly manage that process. Libraries make significant investments in their strategic technology infrastructure. Those with current or future involvement in selecting components of that infrastructure can benefit from this book to gain the knowledge they need to make informed and responsible decisions.

NIKKI WALLER

1
Introduction to the RFP

This chapter explores a traditional request for proposal (RFP) and explains its component parts. Regardless of how you plan to write an RFP, this section outlines the essential information you must share with a vendor, and what you need to request.

SECTIONS OF THE RFP

This chapter presents an outline structure for a typical RFP, developed as a comprehensive statement of requirements for a midsized public library purchasing an integrated library system (ILS). Since this chapter's original publication, library automation has changed significantly in a couple of relevant ways. First, library services platforms have emerged as a new class of product. While the ILS continues to persist strongly in the public library sphere, the

---

Nikki Waller was managing editor for ALA TechSource, 2000–2003.

academic arena has seen a dramatic shift toward the library services platform. The change started through the use of index-based discovery services in tandem with existing ILS, often supplemented by an electronic resource management system. The library services platform diverges considerably from the ILS model, managing print and electronic resources through a more unified, web-native, multi-tenant platform. Chapter 7 covers library services platforms in depth. A second change has been the trend toward resource sharing among libraries, which is covered in chapter 3. Libraries pursue deeper collaborations in collection development, cataloging, and sharing of resources, which are supported by a shared technological infrastructure. Finally, the ILS is increasingly hosted by the vendor or deployed as software-as-a-service.

For each section of the RFP, this chapter also isolates the large questions that the library must ask itself, as well as vendors. You may find sample RFPs to work from, whether from colleagues or posted to the Web. The outline here is only one example of structure. It is meant to guide you in a way of thinking about this initial step in procurement. Even if the details don't apply to your current situation, pay attention to the type of information being shared and gathered.

SECTION I
Instructions to Bidders

This first section is the most narrative and allows the library to tell some of its recent history, as well as outline its plans for the future. This section should explain briefly why the library is seeking a new system, and what functionality it desires from the new system. This section also sets forth basic rules and criteria for the vendor's response.

1. Introduction: Who are you and why are you here?

This item introduces the library to bidders. Create an accurate picture of your library, including the number of holdings, staff members, area population, and registered users. Give vendors a clear idea of the daily life of the library: how many visitors enter each day and analytics on web activity, how many volumes circulate, how many staff members are on duty, and where staff are allocated.

Writers must strike a balance between offering too much detail and being too scant. What should emerge from the introduction is a strong sense of the library's mission and direction, as well as concrete figures about the library's working capacity, facilities, and current systems. Be sure to give a thumbnail sketch of the library's computerized infrastructure as well: how many computers are in use, the networking environment, and what, if any, major hardware purchases are in the offing.

2. Critical requirements: What do you really want?

The essential items that must be present in any bidding vendor's system are listed here. After scanning the list of critical requirements, a vendor should immediately know whether its ILS product meets the library's most basic needs.

Specifications in this item address not only available modules but also alert vendors to what other modules must be supported in the near future. The library states any plans for implementing other capabilities, such as a separate discovery interface. The library also may stipulate that a vendor must be able to support these additional modules in a mandated period of time, usually one year from the contract date. Any other planned expansions in the library's holdings also should be discussed in this section. In addition, the library can set forth rules to guide the demonstration process for the bidding vendor's product.

In this item, you are not seeking to answer questions—the library is giving the vendor the simplest possible definition of what is desired.

3. Scope of the project: What will the new system accomplish?

This section functions as the library's problem statement; if the library seeks to accommodate a growing user population or improve service in a particular way, state it here.

4. The role of the RFP: How does this document work?

This item states what is included in the RFP and how the library weighs each item in its request. The library should provide an explanation of the codes that accompany each requirement. Whether the library uses an RFP based on declarative statements or an RFP based on checklists and open-ended questions, codes give a vendor a clear idea of the library's priorities and how price quotations should be listed in the bid. For example, specifications might be coded with the following symbols:

+ An essential element that is generally available market-wide. The absence of this element is a severe disadvantage.

* A highly desirable element and a major factor in comparing the responses of vendors.

No mark indicates an important element that will be included in the evaluation of responses, but which is not deemed essential or highly desirable.

- An element of interest, but one that would be passed over in favor of a lower bid price. Should be bid as a deduct alternate.

5. Responses to RFP: How to answer the questions

This item indicates how the vendor will mark its response. You may want to warn against vagueness in answers and state that they will be read as negative responses.

6. Exceptions: What does the vendor lack?

If the vendor does not meet the specifications set forth in the RFP, the vendor must specifically address this discrepancy in its proposal.

7. Definitions: What does this mean?

The library clarifies terms that will be used throughout, and how vendors will understand their meaning.

8. Proposal submission: What are the rules of engagement?

The library specifies how the vendor will submit a bid and to whom the vendor can direct questions. Establishing authorized contacts for the vendors within the library is important—all communications with vendors during the bid process should be formal, so that the library does not compromise the terms of the open RFP process. These rules must be specific and clear to both vendors and library staff; the library also indicates penalties and consequences for not adhering to these guidelines.

9. Quantities, appropriation, and delivery: What do the numbers mean?

The library states that quantities listed throughout the RFP are estimates only. These estimates do not guarantee what the library will purchase when a selection is made.

10. Prices: How much?

The library states where and how prices will be listed in the bid, and under what (if any) conditions a vendor may resubmit prices after proposals have been opened.

11. Bid bond: How do we know you're serious?

The library requires that a bond equal to a certain percentage of the bid amount (usually 5 percent) must be submitted with the proposal.

12. Noncollusion affidavit: Will the vendor work independently?

The library requests that vendors adhere to any attached document stating the vendor's intention not to confer with other vendors about the pricing or structure of the bid.

13. Comparison of proposals and discrepancies: What if the numbers don't add up?

If, when comparing products, the library finds a discrepancy between the itemized price and the total price of a system, the library will assume the lowest figure.

14. Nondiscrimination

The library requires that all its contractors fully abide by nondiscriminatory practices.

15. Project schedule: When will the system be ready?

The library requests a detailed project schedule for the first phase of implementation.

16. Guarantees and warrantees: If it breaks, who will fix it?

The library specifies what assurances must be present in its chosen system.

17. Installation: When and how?

The library states that the vendor must abide by specifications for installation listed later in the RFP.

18. Award of contract: How do you know you've won?

This item informs vendors of the procedure for awarding the library system contract.

19. Selection criteria: What is important to the library?

This item plainly explains how the library plans to evaluate bids. Criteria include vendor responsiveness, five-year costs, conformity to standards, past performance of the vendor, and so forth. Discuss any areas of particular concern here. If the viability of a vendor is especially important, the library should explain how it assesses viability (such as the number of installations, financial criteria, and size of development staff).

Some libraries may place importance on a vendor's market strategy, that is, whether the vendor will continue to provide adequate service in the library's market segment. Address those concerns in this item.

20. Rejection of proposals

The library reserves the right to say no to anyone it pleases.

21. Financial statement: Is the vendor healthy?

If the library requires a selected vendor to provide an audited financial statement, stipulate it here.

22. Proposal costs: Who pays for the postage?

The vendor must bear all costs of preparing the proposal and may not pass them along to the library in the bid.

23. Contract: What holds up in court?

This item lists which documents will constitute the legally binding contract between library and vendor (usually the RFP, the vendor's response, the negotiation summary, and any other additional materials).

24. Lease options: What are the other options?

This item requests not only purchase price quotes from the vendor, but system or hardware-only lease prices as well.

Mandatory Proposal Form

The library creates a mandatory proposal form to aggregate basic cost and legal information in a single document. This form helps the library compare between the basic prices of each vendor's product. The bidding vendor must fill out this form, which requests cost breakdowns, discount totals, projected maintenance costs, and delivery dates.

System Requirements

In sections II through VI about system requirements, the library seeks information about a proposed system's functionality. The major question addressed throughout is: can the proposed product accomplish what the library needs?

In the introduction to these sections, the library should define key terms used throughout, explain any symbols that appear, and give vendors instructions to code their responses. Defining and requesting adherence to a standard response code from vendors allows librarians to easily compare responses among vendors. This code also eliminates the possibility of waffling in a vendor's response.

The library also should state what minimum percentage of its specifications (90 to 95 percent is most common) vendors must meet to remain in consideration. These specifications are presented as a numbered list of specifications in the model RFP; modeling many of these specifications into a checklist is a good idea for tightening the document and facilitates easier comparison among vendor responses.

SECTION II
General System Requirements

A. The system: What are you shopping for?

In this section, the library defines the basic traits of the system it seeks: what the procurement consists of, hardware requirements, hosting and models (such as software-as-a-service), installation basics, system size, configurations, speed, supported platforms, web-based interfaces, peripherals, data lines, security, language, training, service, and certain standards. Several of these traits are also specified in more detail later in the RFP, but this section addresses the library's most general needs.

As a mature class of products, nearly all ILS products handily meet basic requirements. Rather than asking vendors what they support, this section can be better constructed as a narrative or bullet-point list that clearly states that these requirements are assumed capabilities of any ILS product.

Checklists also are useful for articulating general requirements. At the end of such a list, however, provide space for the vendor to indicate full compliance with these requests, as well as space for a vendor to explain any gaps in compliance. Vendors need a place to explain their "no" responses; their systems may have eliminated the need in one area by meeting it in another.

B. Modules: What functions are desired?

In this section, the library lays some ground rules for what will be included in the vendor's bid, along with basic assumptions about the bid. ILS systems are increasingly vendor-hosted or delivered through software-as-a-service, and libraries increasingly expect web-based interfaces for both staff and public interfaces. The procurement document should address applicable standards, including MARC21, Dublin Core, RDA, Z39.50, SIP2, NCIP, as well as emerging standards such as BIBFRAME. Libraries should consider what APIs are exposed in the system and the protocol (e.g., REST or SOAP).

The library must specify which modules it seeks and how the modules will be bid. The base bid is the price quote for the system components that the library is certain of purchasing. Below are examples of what might be included in a base bid. See "Additional Resources" at the end of this chapter, which references websites with current RFPs.

- Acquisitions interface to vendor ordering systems, such as GOBI3
- Electronic resource management
- Cataloging interface to bibliographic services, such as OCLC Cataloging, SkyRiver, or other utilities
- Circulation with backup
- Inventorying
- Web-based patron access catalog
- Strategic functionality such as e-book integration
- Report generator
- Any other modules are quoted as options. Modules most commonly quoted as options include:
  - Interlibrary loan tools
  - Enhanced catalog data
  - Enhanced library service products
  - Materials booking
  - Special files
  - Telephone patron notification/renewal
  - Patron self-charging

In this section, the library also asks the vendor for information about any other modules the vendor has in development or in current release. These other modules also should be quoted as options in the vendor's response.

Most libraries are choosing vendor-hosted products or platforms deployed by software-as-a-service, therefore concerns such as required hardware no longer apply. In the past libraries would stipulate that no hardware or software replacement would be needed to accommodate any of the vendor's other modules, and second, any version changes in the library's operating systems should be included in the vendor's maintenance program.

Finally, the library also should request a detailed account of the financial and human resources committed to software development, with a breakdown between staff working exclusively on the ILS and staff working on various companion products.

SECTION III

Detailed Functional Requirements:
Do the System Functions Fit the Library's Needs?

In this section, which is the overwhelming bulk of the RFP, the library tells the vendor precisely what it expects the system to do. These requirements describe the entire function-by-function capability of the ILS.

The model RFP that accompanies this issue extensively covers this territory—in most cases, more than 80 specifications are listed below each function.

These detailed requirements comprise the boilerplate content common to many RFPs. Given the current state of ILS development, the majority of these detailed requirements are now generally accepted in all competitive library management systems:

- Bibliographic file
- Cataloging and authority control
- Acquisitions
- Serials control
- Circulation
- Inventorying
- Patron access catalog
- Interlibrary loan (often quoted as an option)
- Information and referral file
- Materials booking (often quoted as an option)
- Special indexes and files (often quoted as an option)
- Management reports
- Report generator
- Interfacing and network capabilities

SECTION IV

Minimum Hardware Requirements

In this section, the library tells the vendor what hardware configurations the system must work with.

A. General conditions: What hardware runs the library system well?

The library describes its database size in detail (such as the number of bibliographic records, annual interlibrary loan totals, number of registered patron population) as well as a projected expansion size (usually 25 to 30 percent) that the proposed product must accommodate.

The library also asks the vendor for sets of technical and user documentation, and outlines conditions for upgrades to accommodate additional concurrent users.

B. Backup hardware, library data, and redundancies

The library requests information about the disaster planning and recovery process in place.

The library also requests that any proposed system protect the library's data. What are the provisions for redundancy and data replication?

C. Remote peripherals: How will the system work with the library equipment?

The library asks the vendor to provide minimum requirements for staff PCs, web-based patron access catalogs, side printers, etc.

SECTION V

Vendor Support

Vendor support specifications must be the most carefully worded section in the RFP. In this section, the library outlines the vendor's responsibilities for installing and supporting the system. This part of the RFP sets the stage for the working relationship between the vendor and the institution; the library should be explicit in its expectations and requests. By the same token, the library also must confirm it can conform to these guidelines and fulfill its duties.

A. Vendor viability: Is the vendor healthy?

Someone on the library's procurement team should have already conducted a general viability study of vendors in the market, so the library should have a basic idea of any vendor's financial situation. For an official confirmation of viability, the library requests information about the vendor's operations and customers, including audited financial data, résumés of the vendor's project staff, and a complete listing of the vendor's installations from the last four years.

B. Database migrations: How will the transfer work?

The library outlines what it will provide the vendor for the transfer of the library's database and then succinctly lists the vendor's responsibilities, including what hardware the vendor must provide. The library also specifies the initial load size for the database transfer and requests a quote for migrating the library's other records.

C. Delivery and installation: What will the installation process look like?

The library describes, point by point, the delivery and installation process of the new ILS, indicating the library's own responsibilities as well as the vendor's. Because the RFP is a legally binding document, the library procurement team (as well as the library's attorney) must carefully review this section before sending the RFP.

D. Training: How much instruction does the library need from the vendor?

The library indicates how many systems operators will be trained at the vendor's headquarters and specifies what capabilities the systems operators must have after training. The library also outlines how much training the vendor must conduct on-site for other key library personnel. The library requests additional materials from the vendor for training other staff in-house.

E. Maintenance: After installation, what are the vendor's duties?

This section of the document should be prepared in concert with the library's information technology (IT) administrator to determine how much maintenance to request from the vendor and how much can be performed in-house.

The library defines what levels of maintenance the vendor must be responsible for, what hours field maintenance will be available, and what conditions the vendor must meet for repairs.

F. Escrow agreement: What if . . . ?

To protect itself from vendor bankruptcy or cessation of product support (usually measured by the frequency of product releases—if the vendor does not release any update to the product for one year, the product is unsupported), the library asks the vendor to provide or place in escrow the source code and system documentation for all applications. In exchange, the library agrees to sign any nondisclosure agreement provided by the vendor.

The library also stipulates that the application software will be written to permit maintenance by other than vendor personnel in the event that the vendor enters bankruptcy or the product is no longer supported.

SECTION VI

Acceptance and Ongoing Reliability

This section tells the vendor how the library will assess the success of the product installation, and it outlines the vendor's responsibilities after the system has been installed.

A. Components of acceptance: Does the system pass the test?

The library lists the components of its acceptance tests for the system. The library also can reserve the right to withhold payments until after acceptance tests have been successfully conducted. In the event of repeated failures, the library can stipulate the return of all payments and enter into arbitration against the vendor. The system also may be subject to reliability tests as long as two years after initial installation—failure of those tests can result in withholding of maintenance payments.

B. Methodology: What's on the test?

The library gives parameters for the acceptance test, such as how many concurrent users will be included, how system response times will be measured, and how test results will be logged.

C. Reliability and downtime: Is the system there when the library needs it?

The library gives its definition of a reliable system, as well as how reliability will be calculated. The library also defines downtime and describes how it will calculate overall system downtime.

D. Response times: What speed constitutes great service?

How fast does the system need to work? In this section, the library gives minimum rates of response for different system operations (for example, charge and discharge of library materials should average two seconds at least 95 percent of the time) and stipulates that these times must be met even when the maximum number of concurrent users (specified in the general hardware requirements) is using the system.

E. Withholding of maintenance payments: What happens when the system fails?

If the system fails to function at the contracted level of performance, the library reserves the right to withhold a percentage of its regular maintenance payments. Conditions that allow for payment withholding can include:

- Failure to meet reliability rates after acceptance tests have been passed
- Failure to meet required response times
- Loss of files or databases due to system failure

STANDARDS

In 2003 the National Information Standards Organization (NISO) published "The RFP Writer's Guide to Standards for Library Systems," a comprehensive inventory of information standards and how to include them in the library's RFP. Even though not current with the latest standards, this continues to be an excellent guide. Created by Cynthia Hodgson, it includes specifications that can be added to RFPs, as well as explanations of which standards are appropriate for different library projects. See www.niso.org/publications/press/RFP_Writers_Guide.pdf.

ADDITIONAL RESOURCES

Marshall Breeding's Library Technology Guides website has a "Procurement" center where many RFPs are available for download as they're announced: http://librarytechnology.org/procurement.

You might also check the following resources:

Colorado Department of Education, "Request for Proposal (RFP) page," www.cde.state.co.us/cdelib/technology/atrfp.htm.

TechSoup connects nonprofits, foundations, and libraries with tech products, services, and learning resources, and provides tips and sample RFPs for your nonprofit, charity, or library. See www.techsoup.org/support/articles-and-how-tos/rfp-library.

The consortium Orbis Cascade Alliance has posted RFP documents and process information at https://oldsite.orbiscascade.org/index/rfp.

CONCLUSION

Above all, the RFP is a document that seeks information about solving the library's problems or expanding its services. The RFP outline presented here is one way to organize a request for bids, and its areas of functionality are commonly addressed in RFPs for an ILS.

The next chapter, again using an ILS example, discusses how to incorporate your library's needs and desires into a well-written document that will help you achieve successful technology implementation.

2
Writing the RFP

A request for proposal presents a library with a golden opportunity for solving some or all of its problems. The RFP doesn't just explain the library to vendors—it's a valuable tool for communication within the library, too. This example assumes the purchase of an integrated library system (ILS). No matter what the technology product and services you seek, the RFP writer's task is to understand the functionality and apply it to the library's needs and mission.

At its best, an RFP helps a library obtain meaningful information for making purchase decisions. At its worst, an RFP yields canned responses brimming with sales-speak. The RFP is only one part in a dynamic purchase process that includes vendor demonstrations, site visits, and meetings—answers on paper cannot accurately convey the look, feel, and intuitiveness of a system.

This chapter discusses each step in the RFP writing process, focusing on ways to ask intelligent questions.

Nikki Waller was managing editor for ALA TechSource, 2000–2003. An earlier version of this chapter was published in *Library Technology Reports* (July/August 2003).

MAKING A STATEMENT

Although several staff members will contribute to the content of the RFP, the library's purchase team should appoint one person to write the first draft and final document. Working with a single writer ensures that the staff's varying specifications will be translated into a consistent format and language throughout the document.

As he or she begins the first draft, the writer should have materials gathered during the purchase planning process, including the final document from the library's needs assessment, as well as any goal or problem statements. These agreed-upon goals serve as the backbone for the entire purchase, as well as making the task of writing the RFP easier.

In addition to stated goals, the writer also should begin with a clear picture of the library's priorities: what does the library want to accomplish with this purchase, and at what cost? Which library operations cannot be affected or inhibited by the new system? The writer, as well as the entire purchase team, must share a vision of which procedures and workflows may change and what systems cannot change.

By this point, the purchase committee has already held several staff meetings to discuss the upcoming RFP and system purchase. As the purchase team and the writer prepare for the RFP, however, they should appoint representatives from different library units to discuss particular problems or areas for improvement in their units. Some of these concerns may already be addressed in the library-wide goals statement, but others may be unique to certain units. The writer and each representative should work together to develop system specifications for his or her unit.

During the initial draft process, the RFP writer should stay in close contact with unit representatives, as well as technical staff, administrators, purchasing officers, and contract specialists. The RFP is developed in concert with all these personnel, and the writer must adequately address their concerns in the finished document. To accurately represent each department, frequent— but not constant—communication is necessary.

As the writer drafts the first version of the RFP, questions will invariably arise about the particular specifications of each library unit, but refrain from bombarding library staff with dozens of individual inquiries. Instead, the writer should schedule a regular appointment each week (or every few days) for addressing his or her questions with pertinent staff members.

This approach will further convince staff that the RFP writing effort is organized. Staff will be happy to answer a set of questions at regular intervals and will budget time accordingly. (For most people, receiving one e-mail message with eight questions every Thursday afternoon is preferable to receiving eight e-mail messages with one question each throughout the week.) Limiting RFP-related queries to designated periods also helps the writer track which questions have been answered, and when—eliminating the need to ask the same question twice.

At this point in the preparations, the RFP writer and members of the purchase team should issue internal guidelines regarding contact between staff and vendor personnel before, during, and after the RFP is issued. Once word gets out (as it invariably will) that your library is assembling an RFP, expect unsolicited contact from some vendors' sales representatives.

When issuing an open RFP, the library must carefully monitor its contact with vendors to avoid compromising the open RFP process—if a library appears to favor a vendor or if the open RFP seems to explicitly specify one vendor's system, another vendor may challenge the legality of the open RFP process.

Although such instances are rare, a vendor is legally permitted to seek punitive damages against the library. A set of clear ground rules ensures that all communication between vendors and library staff is well-documented and fully aboveboard.

Evaluation Criteria

Before drafting the RFP, the writer and the library purchase team must establish criteria and methodology for evaluating vendor proposals. A solid evaluation plan should contain:

- An explanation of how criteria are weighted
- A description of the library's methodology
- An explanation of the finalist selection process
- Requirements for any demonstrations to follow
- Any requirements for site visits and contact with a vendor's current customers
- A list of minimum conditions that must be met for consideration of a product

In assigning weight to criteria, proceed carefully. The criteria should faithfully reflect the library's priorities (as established during needs assessment or in goal statements). All too often, evaluation criteria are weighted heavily on the most arcane or difficult specifications in an RFP.

Choose what really matters to your library. If the library's first priority is to provide remote patron authentication without disturbing other systems, the most heavily weighted criteria should reflect that. Don't give weight to system attributes that are of little importance to your library—a problem that frequently arises when libraries copy boilerplates used by another institution.

A description of the library's evaluation methodology should include an explanation of the point system the library uses (if any) to tabulate answers and any other information that goes into the process of comparing responses.

If your RFP includes open-ended questions that do not result in yes or no-type responses, thoroughly explain how those responses will be assessed and included in any point totals.

If you plan to use open-ended or short essay-style questions in your RFP, consult the library's attorney or purchasing officer after drafting your library's methodology statement to ensure that the evaluation method is legally solid. The easiest way to evaluate essay-style responses is to assign point values to responses and include a brief schema that explains what constitutes each point value (for example, a short essay-style response that receives one point out of five fulfills only one of five possible requirements).

As any attorney will attest, using strict, numerically based methods of evaluation (such as scorecards) removes the possibility for ambiguity or bias. Such concerns primarily affect public institutions, which frequently operate under rigid government-mandated procurement processes.

The finalist selection process, in which the library chooses which vendors will be invited to demonstrate their system, also should be based on the numerical outcomes of the RFP evaluation. Many libraries state that the three vendor responses with the largest point totals will automatically be considered finalists.

Demonstration, site visit, and customer contact requirements also should be carefully prepared. Think about how much time to give vendors for demonstrations, whether you wish to provide vendors with a demonstration checklist beforehand, and which vendor personnel you want to participate in the site visit.

Minimum requirements usually indicate a certain percentage of the RFP specifications that must be met (95 percent is common) for a system to warrant the library's consideration. The library also can list certain basic functions (for example, a circulation module) that must be present in any considered system.

TIPS FOR WRITING THE RFP

Are We There Yet?

As the writing process begins in earnest, scan the Web to see what's out there—many libraries post their system RFPs. Read through available requests to see what approaches are used and which ones your library should emulate.

Contacting several similar libraries should yield a handful of RFPs to look through.

After you collect information and are overwhelmed by the size of the task at hand, take a breath (or a coffee break). Remember, your library's RFP doesn't have to be tedious. The RFP is an opportunity to find solutions to library problems or to improve your library's service, workflow, or effectiveness.

A CAVEAT BEFORE YOU COPY AND PASTE

After absorbing a few RFPs, one thing will be clear—there's a lot of boilerplate out there. Although you may be tempted to copy another RFP wholesale, don't. Vendors have seen the boilerplate, and bid writers can respond to it in their sleep. If you want a vendor's product to help achieve the unique goals or address the special concerns of your library, then write a unique, original RFP.

After establishing basic functional requirements, an RFP can pose challenging, interesting questions. Even if your library is limited by strict rules governing procurement and purchasing, you can combine standard RFP specifications with provocative questions. Speak with your library's procurement officer to find out how much flexibility you have in the document.

SOME NOTES ON LANGUAGE

Because an RFP is a legally binding document, and because it specifies precise needs and functions, an RFP must be carefully worded. Follow these tips before you begin writing:

Use all-or-nothing terms sparingly. Words such as *must* have especially heavy legal weight and should be used infrequently. Terms such as *highly desirable* or *should* are far less legally problematic and will convey your point nonetheless.

Require vendors to respond specifically—relating how their system will operate in *your* library when describing the library environment and workflow. Responses should explicitly address your library's functional needs and strategic priorities.

Tell vendors about your library and ask how their systems will perform throughout the RFP. Many RFPs consist exclusively of declarative statements, giving a vendor few chances, if any, to explain how its product may be especially suited to your library's needs.

Avoid ambiguity. Each specification should be clear. If you are unsure how to word some specifications, check with any appropriate unit representatives.

Needs, not wants. Avoid the temptation to include functionality that your library does not explicitly need. It is tempting to list functionality seen in other RFPs, but in some cases that functionality can be a relic of outdated practices and is no longer relevant to current library operations.

Avoid copying another institution's RFP wholesale. Not only will a copied RFP fetch unoriginal responses, but many consultants copyright RFPs that they have created. To avoid copyright infringement and numerous other ills, use other RFPs as guides only, customizing your request to your library's needs.

Resist your inner Charlton Heston. A handy rule of thumb as you write the RFP: if a specification reads like something Moses may have found etched on stone tablets (for example, "the vendor shall not be considered viable in the event of the following conditions forthwith"), rewrite it.

Introduction and Scope

The first part of the RFP introduces your library and its mission. The scope of the RFP tells vendors which goals the library hopes to attain by implementing a new system. Begin writing a quick narrative sketch of your library (since this is the first draft, you can revise later). Try to convey basic facts of the library—its size, holdings, user population, major activities—in 300 words or less. Make sure to include any library functions that are particular to your library (for instance, if the library has the largest special collections department in your state).

The introductory section should also include a clear explanation of how responses will be evaluated (covered earlier in this chapter), deadlines and instructions for bids, and a short description of the library's contract practices.

Defining the scope of the RFP not only takes the library's broad concerns into account but also sets basic parameters for the planned system purchase. This section tells vendors what the library expects from the system purchase. One technique for writing this part of the RFP answers the following questions:

Who? Present the basic information about the library and its users, as indicated above.

What? Discuss what the library wants to accomplish with the proposed system, and state the basic functionality that is sought.

When? Provide a rough timetable for implementation, including beta and acceptance testing.

Where? Indicate where the library wants to see improvements—such as better workflow and design features or an easier patron interface. Also describe the size of the library's database, where it is hosted, who owns the content, and any expectations for growth.

Why? Explain the changes or problems that predicate the search for a new system.

How? Specify any deliverables, as well as basic technical configurations.

Several other basic considerations are briefly discussed in these first sections of the RFP.

Developing Smart Specifications

There are no systems out there that don't check out a book,
so why are we still asking whether they do?
—Susan Baerg-Epstein, library consultant.
(Telephone conversation, March 23, 2003)

In earlier stages of ILS development, the multitudes of functional requirements in an RFP actually *did* something—not every system had the full complement of functions and features, and these requirements allowed libraries to assess which systems had the largest amount of desired functionality.

These copious requirements also were used to dare vendors into developing something—RFPs were, in part, libraries' wish lists for features and functions. These wish list functions were used to drive system development. Libraries asked for features several times, in hopes that a vendor would finally bite.

In the current ILS marketplace, where all systems have nearly identical, fairly robust basic functionality, virtually every system can satisfy basic functional requests. The sharpest differences between systems are generally found in each system's approach (including information and database architecture), look and feel, ease of use, and intuitiveness.

The vintage-style RFP is useful only for libraries that have not yet automated their catalog, or for libraries that have not updated their automated system for decades. For all other libraries (which are likely more familiar with the state of library system functionality), such a grandiose effort is not necessary. This section suggests efficient ways to construct listings of functional requirements. While we address the ILS in this chapter, other library technology products may in fact be in these earlier stages. How mature is the technology that you want bids for? What functionality can be assumed? What are your reach functions? Are they viable? How important are they?

Checklists

If the library's purchase team has thoroughly researched the current ILS marketplace, the team members will almost certainly have come to the same conclusion: nearly all ILS products meet all basic requirements for functionality.

If your library's procurement rules permit, listing functional requirements in a checklist is a recommended and efficient strategy for affirming basic attributes of systems. By using a checklist as part of the RFP, the bid writers' jobs are simplified—they can instead focus their energies on responding to the substantial questions in the RFP. Bear in mind, however, that checklists should only be used for baseline functions—features common to all vendors' ILS products.

If your library's procurement rules limit the use of checklists in RFPs, developing specifications in checklists for the first draft can be useful. The specifications in checklists should be short and clearly written, with no room for ambiguity or misinterpretation.

After circulating the first draft of the RFP with checklists, the writer can be sure that he or she has accurately conveyed the library's functional needs. Once that draft is approved, the RFP writer can translate each checklist item into the approved format for individual specifications.

Many libraries that send out RFPs with checklists send them out in Microsoft Excel or other spreadsheet formats. If all you send is a checklist, the format would be fine—chances are, however, that the checklists will be combined with meatier requests for vendor input. Spreadsheet formats create headaches for bid writers, who must tweak the spreadsheet to fit in long answers to questions.

Sending an RFP in two portions (for example, one in Microsoft Word, the other in Excel) or inserting a table into a Word document saves time as well as effort. When choosing a format for the RFP, keep it simple. Ask whether you'd rather the bid writer spend his or her time manipulating spreadsheet cells to squeeze in responses or actually *writing* thoughtful responses.

HOW TO ASK SMART QUESTIONS

Above all, be specific about what the library wants to know. Clearly explain the library's workflows and connect questions about system functionality to their role in the library environment. By tailoring the questioning to the library's needs and concerns, you'll force vendors to tailor their responses in kind.

Know your library's strengths—what systems should not change as the new ILS is adopted? If certain systems cannot be disturbed, ask vendors to explain *how* their ILS can operate around or in harmony with the library's crucial processes and systems, and not just *whether* their ILS can co-operate.

Most questions about existing systems concern the information technology (IT) department. Find out what the technical staff needs to know about the underlying architecture to properly evaluate vendor responses. In the same vein, the RFP writer must have (or must develop) a good working knowledge of how IT systems work in the library in order to ask intelligent questions. In composing the RFP, the writer should have diagrams or basic documents from the IT department so that the specifications make sense to the writer and result in clear statements.

SCENARIOS

The use of scenarios in RFPs has become increasingly popular, but be judicious in their use. Scenarios give the library a rich picture of a system in action and allow greater insight into how systems operate than do simple yes or no questions.

All too often, however, scenarios merely ask questions that the library will ask again during a vendor's product demonstration. If the question seeks to actually see the system, put it aside for any demonstration scripts that will be developed.

In addition, RFP writers frequently pose overly specific scenarios. A poorly written scenario asks something like: A professor and a student place a hold on a book from different remote locations at the exact same time. To whom does the system give the hold, and how does it convey the appropriate messages? In all likelihood, the vendor will explain that the server accepts requests in hundredths of a second, so such simultaneous situations are virtually impossible. But the library really wanted to know whether and how the system gives priority to certain users and how ensuing notification works.

Well-written scenarios allow the vendor to explain its system and why it's ideal for your library. Scenarios should describe expected events—power outages, lost records, conflicting hold requests—not freak occurrences. Stay focused on obtaining meaningful information from scenarios, and resist the temptation to make vendors squirm and scramble to find answers for next-to-impossible (and next-to-meaningless) questions.

AVOIDING PITFALLS

The task of writing and issuing a successful RFP is not terribly complex or difficult, but does call for careful planning and sensible, specific requirements. The following list discusses the most common pitfalls in the RFP writing process:

Not enough time is spent on vendor education. Not all vendors are created equal. A vendor's greatest fear is that a solution has already been chosen [by the institution] and that it is wasting its time. This [situation] manifests itself when the RFP inadvertently favors a technology or solution because the team had the most education on that particular technology.

Poorly defined requirements. This [problem] is typically due to two basic reasons. First, see the item above. Second, not enough time is spent understanding and documenting the [institution's] internal requirements . . . requirements are so broadly stated as to be meaningless to a vendor. A recent RFP requested that the [system] support output to different formats and devices. When questioned [by the vendor] as to what was meant, the buyer compounded the mistake by requiring that the [system] support not only current formats, but also any future formats that may be developed within the industry! ("Wow, so I might as well file for Chapter 11 right now and get it over with," said one would-be vendor respondent.)

Poor coordination among key stakeholders. Did you forget to bring in the test group until after the contract was awarded? In one RFP, much time was spent on describing developers, administrators, the IT department, but almost no time was spent describing the actual users of the system—the people who would use the system to obtain the information they needed. When vendors questioned the RFP team about the "users of the system" the RFP team could not adequately define who a user was, what a user would do on the system, how many users there were, how many hits were expected, what the average length of time spent on the site would be, and so forth. In their haste to completely define the "solution," the RFP team forgot the audience.

Providing requirements that can't be adequately defined and therefore proposed. This [problem] typically involves using [ambiguous or impossible] requirement statements . . . [another] common mistake is to require something like "all products should conform to all AIIM content management standards . . ." Without defining the specific standard or set of standards, many vendors will be absolutely clueless as to which standards they meet and which ones they don't meet. (Hence this typical response: "Oh, to hell with it, say we meet them all—they'll never check anyway.") Given ambiguous or unclear requirements, most vendors will simply say yes, and if questioned will bring out all the issues involved and make the matter so complex that it will never be resolved. This method is in the spirit of "better to beg forgiveness than ask permission," because once a vendor has been selected . . . little chance [exists] that they will be unselected.

(Text excerpted from "The Case for RFPs (When done right . . .)," by Bud Porter-Roth. Published by Content Management System Watch, May 14, 2002, at www.cmswatch.com.)

TIPS FROM BID WRITERS

Poorly written RFPs don't just hurt libraries, they also tarnish the working lives of vendor bid writers, the staff charged with responding to RFPs. Generally speaking, bid writers don't like responding to age-old boilerplates any more than libraries like writing them. No one wants to prevent the library from receiving the information it seeks. All too often, the library just needs to learn to ask questions more carefully.

Nicole Lemley-Rautama, bids and marketing coordinator with Ex Libris (USA), gives the following four suggestions. [*Editor's Note:* Communications options have expanded dramatically since these remarks. We run them verbatim because they are still relevant in the spirit. Respect the vendor's time and costs by making the response process as efficient as possible.]

The cost of producing paper RFP responses is incredible. One binder alone can cost more than $5. Multiply that by the requisite five copies, add printing and tab costs, shipping, and several responses in one year and the cost is immense. Although we ostensibly provide these copies free for libraries, the cost is built in somewhere—in software, maintenance, and so on. Let's explore alternative formats for RFP delivery. CD-ROMs are inexpensive to produce and ship.

Standards, and "standards." Standards compliance is a complex issue, much more so than simply ticking yes or no to a question such as, "Do you comply with Z39.50?" There's a matter of complying with all variations of Z39.50, not just one portion which enables a vendor to say yes. Not only should libraries care about standards compliance, but how it is accomplished and to what depth. How is the vendor involved in standards creation and compliance?

Bidder's conferences. We don't want them eliminated, but we'd like to see them become telephone conferences. These on-site conferences take an enormous amount of time, effort, and money (once again that ultimately comes from the libraries' pockets) to attend said meetings, which sometimes last no more than 30 minutes.

Libraries, please include an electronic copy—in word processing format, most usually MS Word, of your RFP. This RFP will become the basis, in turn, for our response. Answers will be integrated into the original document, and the original will be saved separately, unscathed. This format makes the vendor's response that much more efficient.

Bid writers and marketing personnel from Endeavor and GIS Information Systems (formerly Gaylord Information Systems) contributed the following tips to improve the library RFP experience. (Data collected through phone interviews March through May 2003.)

- "We see a *lot* of overkill regarding standards. Z39.50 and MARC 21 are included. Stop asking about them."

  Lots of space is consumed in the RFP by specifying, standard by standard, what a system should support. To save time and space, list the standards the system should comply with. The overwhelming majority of libraries seek support for the exact same standards, which are all included in virtually every ILS. Allow a vendor space to indicate or explain why a particular standard is not supported. (Here's one way to phrase the question: Does your system include support for all the following standards? If not, please identify and explain.)

- "If you're working with a consultant, insist on originality in the RFP. After all, you're paying for it."

  Many library consultants have been using the same RFPs for years, and bid writers can easily identify the boilerplates of different consultants. If an RFP has been past the vendor often enough, the bid department already has an MS Word document with the answers, and the writer plugs them right in.

- "Don't ask us to explain how we plan to support your hardware environment and expect the response to fit in a spreadsheet cell."

  Libraries often require vendors to format their responses in complicated and strange ways. Such format requirements are understandable for public institutions, whose state or government authorities maintain rigid styles for procurement documents, but in other cases, a library's formatting requests seem somewhat arbitrary. Nonetheless, says one bid writer, "We jump through the hoops. We have to."

- "If you want a thoughtful response, then give us time to think."

  Provide ample time in which to prepare a good bid response. Thirty days should be the minimum turnaround; 45 is preferable. Bid writers observe that many RFPs arrive with 7- to 14-day turnarounds, and note that providing a high-quality response in such a limited time is extremely difficult.

- "Don't ask for the moon unless you're at least somewhat sure we offer it as an option."

  If you're willing to spend the money on a product, develop a realistic idea of what it can do. This problem mainly arises in RFPs for new products such as portals or federated search systems. Librarians who send RFPs for these products frequently haven't learned enough about the products as a class. The RFP is intended to gain specific information about a specific type of product, but do due diligence first: find out, in a general way, what's out there.

Vendors receive pie-in-the-sky proposals with wild expectations—a clear sign to the vendor that you don't know what you want. As a result, the vendor is less likely to take you seriously. In these bids, writers spend a lot of time discussing the realities of the systems and what's possible today. Recognize that anything may be possible in the future, but first address what's possible now.

- "Know what you want."

  The greatest barrier to a good RFP is that libraries send out bid boilerplates without placing priorities on the functions they want, which is especially true of libraries that work with consultants. A library should know what it's asking for, and it should be sure that every specification in the RFP is something it cares about.

Libraries often copy other RFPs wholesale from another source, but the copied RFP may contain specifications that matter little to the library. When a vendor doesn't support some of those specifications, the library eliminates a vendor based on something it didn't need—resulting in a doubly bad situation because the library may have eliminated the most suitable vendor, and it may end up paying for something superfluous.

Every question is important in terms of the inclusion and exclusion of potential vendors. At the start of the process, the library should be inclusive—you don't want to unnecessarily eliminate a product that might be an excellent match.

The vendor may not bid at all on your project if it can't meet all your specifications. If you've specified something of little to no importance to the library and several vendors can't live up to it, the library will have fewer options to choose from.

Bid writers also contributed a few tips that require little explanation:

- Include the due date and time clearly at the beginning of the proposal.
- Provide a clear, complete address for delivery—not a P.O. box (FedEx and other rapid couriers do not deliver to P.O. boxes).
- Clearly define how many copies of the response are needed and in what format.

- Specify for what period of time the proposal must be valid (preferably in the pricing section).
- Provide an electronic version of the RFP in an editable format; Microsoft Word is preferred.
- Ask for something once, and only once. Many RFPs arrive with a considerable duplication of requirements, slowing the response process.

3
Introduction to Resource Sharing

No library today can be expected to directly hold all of the resources to fulfill all the needs of its users. Rather, most libraries supplement their local collections through resource-sharing arrangements that allow them to offer their clientele access to a broader universe of materials. Libraries participate in local, regional, or global services for the borrowing and lending of materials, supported by different types of organizational relationships and technical infrastructure.

In these times when libraries experience harsh budgetary limitations, they need to exploit every possible opportunity to achieve better services for their patrons with fewer resources. Interlibrary loan, consortial borrowing, document delivery, and shared collections are some of the key strategies that allow libraries to provide access to more materials than are available in their local collections. Books involve the fulfillment of a physical object that must be returned to its original owning institution; articles, book chapters, and

An earlier version of this chapter was published in *Library Technology Reports* (January 2013).

other content items of manageable length can be scanned for electronic delivery. Different types of technical infrastructure are needed to support each of these models of resource sharing. Material type plays a major role in resource-sharing options.

CONCEPTS AND OPTIONS

Many different models are found within the realm of resource sharing. We will consider global interlibrary loan services such as OCLC's WorldShare Interlibrary Loan service, as well as systems that facilitate cooperative reciprocal lending among consortia or regional library systems to more effectively pool and share their collections.

The key principle of resource sharing centers on enabling libraries to provide access for their patrons to materials beyond their immediate local collection. Some involve reciprocal agreements where libraries make some or all of their collections available on request to patrons affiliated with cooperative partner institutions; others, where libraries or other organizations supply materials for a fee.

Technology plays an essential role in support of resource sharing. Libraries depend on various types of automation systems to manage their collections, and other layers of infrastructure are needed to enable the broader exchange of resources among libraries and their patrons. Some of the important areas that we will examine include staff workflow tools that help personnel in a library manage requests and fulfillments from external systems; system-to-system communications that allow integrated systems to interact with resource-sharing environments, supporting standards, or protocols; and other technology or infrastructure components. We will consider some of the models of resource sharing, ranging from circulation of materials within a single library system, to consortial borrowing environments created among libraries with independent integrated library system implementations, to centralized interlibrary loan services, to shared infrastructure in support of automation and resource sharing.

BEYOND CIRCULATION

Resource sharing goes beyond local circulation—the lending of materials owned by the library to its own directly affiliated clientele. Local circulation in itself can be a fairly complex operation, with business rules designed to maximize equitable access to library materials. Circulation systems need the ability to determine whether or not an item can be borrowed by any given category of patron, the length of circulation periods, whether renewals are allowed, and what fines or other measures apply when materials are returned late or lost. A circulation system routinely includes the ability to allow a patron to place holds on items of interest that might not be immediately available and to be notified when it is ready for pickup. Multibranch facilities usually allow patrons to borrow materials from any branch in the system, using the holds feature. These libraries would have procedures in place to route materials from one branch to another to fulfill these requests. The circulation of materials within a single library, even if it operates multiple branches, is a well-understood process and can be managed through the built-in functionality of most integrated library systems. Costs for lending items within a library system are low since the routing of materials involves relative short distances and can be handled through in-house or contracted couriers. In most cases, no additional transaction or service fees apply.

Routine circulation provides efficient access to the materials a library owns. The key limitation, however, lies in the finite nature of library collections. Access to a broader universe of materials requires business and technical arrangements with external services.

NATIONAL AND GLOBAL INTERLIBRARY LOAN SERVICES

A long-standing model of interlibrary loan involves a centralized service that brokers requests among very large groups of libraries. OCLC stands as the best-known and largest organization providing this type of service. In previous times, several other services existed, including UTLAS in Canada, Western Library Network (WLN) based in Washington, and Research Libraries Information Network (RLIN), but considerable consolidation has transpired over the last two decades. WLN and RLIN have become part of OCLC, and the former UTLAS services have been subsumed within Auto-Graphics. Many national libraries, including those of Australia, New Zealand, and most countries in Europe, operate centralized interlibrary loan services. Others, such as CISTI in Canada, Docline, operated by the National Library of Medicine, and the British Library operate large-scale document delivery services.

Centralized interlibrary loan services are often tied to bibliographic services, such as the maintenance of a comprehensive bibliographic database that provides MARC records in support of original and copy cataloging. As part of the bibliographic services, either through online cataloging or through batch processes, holdings data is associated with the MARC records in support of related services, including interlibrary loan.

These interlibrary loan services play an essential role in the global enterprise of resource sharing. Almost any desired item, no matter how obscure or rare, can be provided through one of these services. OCLC's WorldCat, for example, aggregates metadata describing massive amounts of material available on request.

The main disadvantages of this model of interlibrary loan involve high expense and relatively long times to fulfill requests. Costs might include transaction fees assessed by the interlibrary loan service broker, charges assessed by the lender, and shipping. A request might cycle through multiple potential suppliers before it is completed, and shipping from distant locations will extend the fulfillment interval even further. Yet for materials that cannot be supplied in other ways, these services play a vital role.

Some of the technology issues related to these centralized interlibrary loan systems include the standards, pragmatic protocols, application programming interfaces (APIs), and other techniques for automated submission, tracking, and monitoring of requests and workflow tools that streamline the business processes associated with submission and fulfillment of requests.

CONSORTIAL RESOURCE SHARING

Libraries also engage in other arrangements that can satisfy at least some percentage of their patrons' needs at lower costs and with faster fulfillment than a monolithic interlibrary loan service. By banding together in consortia, libraries are able to pool their resources to gain various benefits. The ability to draw from materials distributed across a larger group of libraries can significantly increase the size of the collection effectively available to patrons and reduce the number of requests made to higher-cost services. While these consortial groupings do not offer the comprehensive level of resources available globally, they establish a pool of resources far greater than any of the participating libraries would hold individually. Rather than rely on the postal service or commercial shipping, consortia often implement a courier service that makes regular rounds among the participating facilities.

These consortial resource-sharing organizations depend on some type of technology infrastructure. As shown below, models include sharing an integrated library system or using add-on software that provides discovery and request management in conjunction with multiple integrated library systems that may be in place in the participating institutions.

MANAGING WORKFLOWS

Different types of technology infrastructure are available to support resource sharing within a consortium or to streamline the ways that a library makes use of a centralized interlibrary loan service. Interlibrary loan operations involve a complex set of tasks and workflows that benefit from automation tools that can eliminate or simplify steps. Support for interlibrary loan processing is generally not within the scope of integrated library systems. Yet an important part of the interlibrary loan automation process involves the movement of library materials in ways that require updates or circulation operations within the ILS.

The traditional workflow for processing interlibrary loan requests has been one where library personnel play a direct role. They would perform tasks such as submitting the request to the interlibrary loan service on behalf of the patron, completing and verifying the citation to confirm that that item exists, verifying that it is not available in the local collection, or selecting a set of potential suppliers to fulfill the request. When an interlibrary loan office receives a request for an item, possible workflow steps include verifying that it is held by the library, determining if it is eligible for external loan and whether it is in use, and ultimately retrieving the item from the collection, charging it out in the local circulation system, performing any needed updates in the interlibrary loan system, and then packaging the item and directing it to the appropriate shipping service. Each of these many different possible steps adds time and expense to the process. Different types of technology infrastructure have been developed to eliminate as much staff intervention as possible, to streamline workflows, and to create rapid and less expensive resource-sharing environments.

One of the key tactics in the broader strategy of enabling more efficient resource sharing is to create ways to short-circuit as many of the tasks in the traditional workflow as possible. Any scheme that can eliminate steps of human intervention or mediation should result in faster and less expensive transactions. A more streamlined cycle of workflow for an interlibrary loan transaction might give the patron the tools to efficiently discover materials of interest, capture definitive and accurate citations, and submit valid requests directly to a lender whose ownership of the item has been verified. Achieving these efficiencies depends on technical components that can reliably enable patron requests and route requests along the appropriate chain of potential suppliers, with effective tools for tracking, reporting, and staff intervention as needed.

CONNECTING INCOMPATIBLE SYSTEMS

One of the challenges in resource sharing relates to the different technology platforms involved. An interlibrary loan system relies on a large-scale business application that manages the metadata of available resources, routes requests for materials, and performs a myriad of other activities in support of its operations. Libraries use the circulation module of their integrated library system to manage their inventory of materials and associated lending activities to their own users. The separate operation of these two independent systems can impose a great deal of duplicative work for the users in need of materials, for the interlibrary loan personnel involved, and even for the underlying computer systems.

Finding ways for requests to automatically flow among interlibrary loan systems and integrated library systems is one of the great technology challenges to be solved. International standards, such as ISO ILL or other agreed-upon techniques for the exchange of request transactions between systems and NCIP or SIP for communicating with a circulation module of an ILS, and the use of APIs are part of the toolkit of components available for the construction of a technology environment that can knit systems together seamlessly.

LOAD BALANCING

Cooperative arrangements for resource sharing ideally distribute the workload evenly among participants. Whether a library is a net lender or a net borrower will depend on the relative strength of its collections and the research needs of its patrons. It's also important not to overburden any library disproportionately. The business logic of any resource-sharing or interlibrary loan system needs to be programmed to select potential lenders in ways that balance the load.

TRUSTED SYSTEMS

Efficient resource sharing involves establishing networks of trusted systems in support of the cooperative agreements among institutions. Reciprocal borrowing arrangements establish the general principle that a given set of libraries agree to allow their patrons to borrow materials from each other's collections. The implementation of these agreements requires some supporting technical infrastructure. There are various approaches possible, including those that rely on applications that enable groups of libraries with separate ILS implementations to communicate with each other in support of reciprocal borrowing and others that might involve participating in a shared ILS that can both provide standard automation support for the libraries and facilitate resource sharing. The ability to route requests automatically between peer-to-peer resource-sharing networks or to pass unfulfilled requests to centralized ILL services also involves extending that trusted network to external systems.

DOCUMENT DELIVERY

Document delivery constitutes a major portion of the resource-sharing arena. As opposed to books, which must be physically sent from, and later returned to, the supplying library, requests for journal articles, research reports, individual book chapters, or other items of finite size are fulfilled through a different set of workflows generally known as document delivery. Although there are many variations, the general process involves the lending library fulfilling the request by scanning the requested item and transmitting it electronically to the borrower's library or even directly to the borrower. Document delivery requires specialized technology support applications that may differ significantly from those used for books or other physical materials.

The methods of transmission of documents continue to evolve. Prior to the Internet, the lending library would create photocopies that would be shipped physically. Fax transmission became common beginning in the 1980s and is still used, though rarely. Today most document fulfillment takes place by transmitting scanned documents across the Internet. Specialized applications, such as Ariel from Atlas Systems and Odyssey from Introtrieve, were created that facilitate the efficient exchange of scanned documents among interlibrary loan offices. The document, once received by the borrowing institution, may be printed for pickup by the patron, but it will more likely be delivered through an e-mail attachment or posted to a secured website where it can be downloaded by the patron using campus or library log-in credentials. A recent technique simplifies the process even more by scanning the document directly to cloud-based storage where it can be securely downloaded by the requesting patron. OCLC's Article Exchange service follows this approach.

Document delivery procedures must include steps in the fulfillment that ensure compliance with copyright. The document delivery management system will need to capture, for example, the number of times that each item has been supplied and any other parameters that reflect whether or not an item can be supplied within the guidelines or policies related to copyright compliance. Some libraries may work with services such as those provided by the Copyright Clearance Center to help manage copyright fees.

The fundamental changes related to the electronic publishing of journal content have made a major impact on document delivery services. A very large portion of the journal articles published are now available electronically. Many academic and research libraries now have electronic subscriptions for current issues and back runs of many journals and periodicals and have placed physical copies of those titles in storage. The need to scan articles to fulfill a document delivery request has diminished accordingly.

As libraries shift away from print collections of articles to electronic collections, different business or legal restrictions may apply. The use of electronic resources is governed by license agreements made between the library and a publisher or provider. The terms of these licenses may or may not allow materials to be lent to individuals not directly affiliated with the library. Tracking the eligibility of lending electronic materials adds a new layer of complication to the resource-sharing arena.

In the e-journal realm, libraries face the same reality as with print journals: they are not able to subscribe to all the materials that may be needed by their patrons. Other means to fulfill requests for articles not within the library's subscriptions are available, such as pay-per-article services from the publishers. Libraries continue to provide document delivery services by scanning articles as needed, but they may also be able to lend the electronic copies from their subscribed content resources when allowed by their license terms.

The recent advent of index-based discovery services also has an impact on document delivery. These services, such as Summon or Primo Central from Ex Libris, EBSCO Discovery Service, WorldCat Discovery Service, and especially Google Scholar, provide easy-to-use tools that allow library patrons to gain access to the universe of article-level content. Depending on the search scenario, this might include articles beyond those subscribed to by their home library. These discovery services have the potential to increase demand for document delivery services.

SHARED ILS WITHIN A SINGLE LIBRARY SYSTEM

An ILS shared by a library system provides a shared automation and discovery environment for a group of libraries within the same organization. These libraries operate under a common governance and funding structure. Examples include countywide library systems, library districts, multibranch municipal libraries, and even statewide or national systems. Materials in these shared systems are routinely circulated among all the facilities.

One of the key features related to sharing resources within these types of systems involves the ability to easily transfer items among branches. This capability enables patrons to request and receive materials housed at any facility within the system at the branch most convenient for their use. Traditionally, materials are assigned to specific branches or facilities, and materials delivered to a borrower at another branch are returned to the owning location. Another arrangement allows collection items to float, with items remaining at the branch to which they are returned even if they were originally assigned to another facility. Some libraries implementing floating collections create a layer of business rules that would identify specific items designated to be returned to their home location or that would control overall volume transfers so that the net gain or loss in the total number of materials in any given branch remains within designated thresholds.[1]

The circulation modules of most integrated library systems support floating collections. Some of the products that include this capability are Virtua, Sierra, Millennium, or Polaris from Innovative Interfaces, Library.Solution from The Library Corporation, SirsiDynix Symphony, and SirsiDynix Horizon.

CONSORTIAL SYSTEMS
WITH DISTRIBUTED AUTOMATION SYSTEMS

Many consortia bring together groups of libraries where each operates its own integrated library system. Efficient reciprocal borrowing among libraries with separate integrated library systems requires the implementation of an additional layer of technical infrastructure. This infrastructure would have a variety of components, including a union catalog that spans the collections of the participating libraries, a request management system, and connectors to the ILS of each of the participating libraries.

The basic resource-sharing scenario is to enable a patron to search the collective holdings of the entire consortium, request an item from any of the participating libraries, and have that item delivered to the patron's home library for pickup. While that workflow may be built in to many multibranch ILSs for a single library system, it is more difficult to achieve when multiple ILS implementations are involved, especially a mix of different ILS products.

The union catalog component of the consortial resource-sharing environment can be implemented in different ways. A physical union catalog would consist of a bibliographic database populated with the holdings of each of the participating libraries. The MARC records would be extracted from each ILS instance and loaded into the union catalog system at some periodic interval, maintaining data regarding which library holds each item. Regular ongoing synchronization between the union catalog and local systems is needed to keep data current.

Another option involves using federated search technology, usually based on the Z39.50 protocol, to create a virtual union catalog. Under this approach, the queries entered by patrons would be broadcast to each of the ILS implementations to dynamically identify materials available within the consortium and the owning library. The virtual union catalog approach avoids the overhead of loading and synchronizing MARC records, but it may have limitations in performance and scale.

The consortial resource-sharing system would also include a request management system. Some of its capabilities would include accepting requests via the union catalog or other means, routing the request between ILS implementations of the owning and borrowing libraries, and performing various tracking and management functions. The process is based on using the existing functionality of the circulation module of the ILS to allow a remote borrower to place a hold on an item, which would then be routed to the designated library in the same way as any other local pickup location. The home ILS of the patron likewise exercises the circulation functionality that applies to notifying the patron that the item is available and charging the item to the patron for the specified loan period. The core problem is that the ILS of the library owning the desired item will not have a record for individual patrons of the partner libraries, and the ILS of the borrower's library will not have a bibliographic or holdings record for the requested item. These problems are solved through a series of commands executed by the request management system, using the NISO Circulation Interchange Protocol (NCIP). The sequence would include some variation of these actions:

- A patron associated with Library A places a request for an item in Library B.
- The patron is authenticated as a valid patron eligible to make the request using the patron bar code number and PIN in the ILS of Library A.
- A temporary patron is created on the ILS of Library B.
- A hold transaction is submitted for the item record in Library B and the temporary patron record, specifying the desired pickup location in Library A.
- A temporary item record is created in the ILS of Library A.
- A hold transaction is generated for the patron in Library A against the new temporary item record.
- The circulation module of Library B includes the item in its routine list of materials to be pulled for hold requests.
- The item is physically routed from Library B to Library A.
- Library A receives the item.
- The circulation module of Library A generates a hold notice to the patron indicating the item is available, and it is placed on the hold shelf of the designated branch.
- The item is checked out to the patron using normal circulation procedures, based on pre-established loan rules for loan interval, renewals, and fines.
- The item is returned by the patron and discharged on the ILS of Library A.
- A message is generated to route the item back to Library B.
- Library B receives the item.
- The temporary item and patron records are removed.
- Selected data regarding the transaction is logged for statistical reporting.

While this sequence of actions seems complex and fragile, it can be entirely automated by the request management application and allows the library to handle these consortial loans using the same system and procedures that apply for the circulation of its own materials. Depending on the efficiency of the courier service among the libraries in the consortium, this model of consortial borrowing can make materials available to patrons in times similar to local hold requests. Fulfilling requests in this way is much less expensive than relying exclusively on external interlibrary loan services. Only those requested items not available in any library in the consortium would need to be processed through an external interlibrary loan request. The consortial request management system might optionally have the capability to automatically route such requests using the ISO ILL protocol, an API, or other system-to-system interchange method.

SHARED ILS FOR A LIBRARY CONSORTIUM

A consortium of libraries of independent funding and governance might also join together to participate in a shared integrated library system. Such an arrangement comes with complications beyond an ILS shared among the branches of a library system but avoids the complexities seen above in managing transactions among the circulation modules of multiple ILS implementations. In a consortium, the libraries may have different policies, priorities, and organizational concerns, which all have implications for the shared ILS. Some of the issues that potentially apply to a consortially shared ILS include these:

- Different libraries may have different circulation policies for materials, such as loan periods and fines assessed.
- The interests of participating libraries in emphasizing their branding and identity in online catalog search and display pages may conflict.
- The funding model for an automation environment shared by independent libraries varies, but usually involves distributing costs among participants according to a formula that includes factors such as service population, size of geographic service area, size of collection, or other variables. In some cases, the consortium may be funded centrally by a state agency or other sponsor.
- Materials may be owned by the individual libraries. Though available for borrowing by patrons affiliated with any library in the consortium, returned materials must be routed to the owning facility.

- An ILS shared within a consortium may also include multibranch libraries. The loan rules and other policies for how materials circulate within these groups may be different from those for the overall consortium.

A shared ILS provides opportunities for libraries to gain benefits not just in resource sharing, but also in lowering their overall automation costs. The costs of participating in a shared ILS in almost all cases will be less than the library operating its own implementation. The total expense of operating the system, including the costs for the ILS software and maintenance, hardware, and technical and administrative personnel, can be distributed among consortial participants. A shared ILS also avoids the expense of the add-on consortial borrowing infrastructure. A consortially shared ILS also provides opportunities for other services, such as centralized acquisitions and cataloging. According to Leon and Kress, the cost per transaction in this model averages $3.88, versus $12.11 for traditional interlibrary loan transactions.[2]

Participating in a shared ILS raises various issues of policy and practice. The participating members may elect to adopt a simplified set of circulation policies for loan periods, numbers of allowed renewals, fines, and other operational parameters. A shared ILS, however, would allow each library to maintain separate policies as needed.

An ILS shared by a consortium provides inherent resource-sharing capabilities. Through the use of a common automation infrastructure with a comprehensive database that spans the materials of all the collection members, patrons have access to a large aggregate collection, a much larger pool of materials than any member library could offer individually.

One of the key features of such a consortially shared ILS involves allowing patrons to request materials, either from their own local library or any other library in the consortium, through a simple hold operation as provided through the online catalog and circulation modules. Placing a hold triggers a message to the home library of the item, which is pulled and routed to the requesting library. By using the built-in capabilities of the circulation system, fulfilling a request is inexpensive and fast, depending on the efficiencies of the consortium's courier service among its members.

These ILS implementations shared within a consortium can serve a large number of libraries. One of the ongoing trends involves continual expansion of the size of these shared ILS consortia, often through the consolidation resulting from the mergers of previously separate consortia. In the current era of infinitely scalable computing platforms, the number of libraries that can reasonably share the common infrastructure of an ILS may be virtually unlimited. Ambitions for statewide or national automation infrastructure may be within our grasp.

THE ROLE OF DISCOVERY

Resource-sharing environments often involve a discovery layer that allows library patrons or personnel to search the universe of materials available. Such a discovery layer can take one of several different forms, including the physical and virtual union catalogs discussed above.

One of the major trends in the library technology arena over the last few years has been the development and adoption of discovery environments of ever wider scope. Index-based or "web-scale" discovery services have emerged that search the body of articles and other materials represented within a library's subscriptions to electronic resources in addition to the books and other physical items managed locally. Products in this genre include Summon or Primo Central from Ex Libris, EBSCO Discovery Service, and OCLC's World-Cat Local. Three of these discovery environments—Summon, Primo Central, and EBSCO Discovery Service—are based on indexes maintained by the discovery service provider of electronic content blended with records harvested from the library's local automation system. While this approach has great potential in providing access to articles held by the library and to the broader universe of electronic content, it focuses on the physical materials held by the library. To search for physical items beyond the library's holdings, patrons might need to perform another search in a consortial catalog or WorldCat .org. WorldCat Local has stronger discovery capabilities for physical materials since it intrinsically searches the entire WorldCat database, giving preferential relevance ordering to materials held by the user's home library. Materials not owned by the library and available through interlibrary loan, or in some cases through consortial borrowing, are presented as a standard feature.

A library typically features a search box for its online catalog on its website. Depending on the configuration of the library's automation environment, this search box may provide access to the holdings of the local library system or consortium. To find materials not held within the system, the patron would need to also search any consortial catalogs available or WorldCat.

NOTES

1. Ann Cress, "The Latest Wave," *Library Journal* 129, no. 16 (October 1, 2004), www.libraryjournal.com/article/CA456235.html.
2. Lars Leon and Nancy Kress, "Looking at Resource Sharing Costs," *Interlending & Document Supply* 40, no. 2 (2012): 81–87.

4

Key Standards for Interoperability in Resource Sharing

ny given resource-sharing environment gains flexibility through the ability to communicate with external systems. By their nature, resource-sharing systems need the ability to send and receive information related to the submission of a request and the various possible steps involved in its fulfillment. Interlibrary loan and resource-sharing arenas benefit from standardized protocols for passing messages and requests from one system to another rather than each operating within its own proprietary environment.

Many different resource-sharing scenarios require the interchange of messages, including

- the submission of a request from a local library system to an interlibrary loan fulfillment agency
- the handoff of a request from a regional resource-sharing system to a global interlibrary loan agency

An earlier version of this chapter was published in *Library Technology Reports* (January 2013).

- automated transmission of requests processed by an interlibrary loan office to a fulfillment service
- transfer of requests from discovery services to fulfillment agencies
- communications between integrated library systems and resource-sharing systems to automate the processing of requested materials in the local circulation modules

In support of these automated processes, standards have emerged specifically related to the messaging involved in interlibrary loan requests; existing protocols already in place related to library circulation transactions and discovery are used as well.

ISO ILL

An international standard, ISO 10160 and 10161, commonly called ISO ILL, has been in development for over two decades. It has an interesting history of pioneering development, spotty implementation, and growing obsolescence. The rise and fall of ISO ILL illustrate the long-standing and ongoing need for a standard method to route requests related to ILL among diverse systems as well as the incredible complexity involved.

Canada was the center of pioneering efforts in the peer-to-peer interlibrary loan. During the 1980s, in support of its interlibrary loan service, the National Library of Canada developed a set of messages, or scripts, which could be passed via electronic mail to submit a request or other related operations. This ILL messaging protocol became the Canadian National Standard. In parallel to the Canadian National Standard, the Canada Institute for Scientific and Technical Information, which operated a major document delivery service, created its own message scripts, received via e-mail, to automate requests. This Generic Script Messaging, or GSM, remains in use even today by resource-sharing services in Canada.[1]

The International Organization for Standardization began work in 1991 on a protocol, based on the Canadian National Standard, for interlibrary loan transactions. Following two years of work, the initial version of ISO 10160/10161, generally known as ISO ILL, was published in two parts, the first (10160) dealing with the service definition, and the second (10161) defining the protocol specification and conformance statements. A revision to the protocol was issued in 1997. A third edition of the ISO ILL protocol was developed by the ILL Protocol Implementors Group (IPIG) in 2003 but was not ratified by ISO voting members, mostly due to concerns that it was not backwardly compatible with previous versions. Version 2 remains as the current standard. In 2007 ISO reaffirmed Version 2 of the ILL standard for an additional five years. Collections Canada serves as the maintenance agency for the ISO standard.[2]

With the formalization of the standard, a number of systems began incorporating it to transport requests for resources to external systems or services, but the number of systems supporting the protocol was never especially large. As we will see in the following section, some of the systems that currently support the ISO ILL protocol include OCLC's WorldCat Resource Sharing system, Auto-Graphics ShareIT, Relais ILL, and VDX. The standard is used by the national interlibrary loan systems in Canada, New Zealand, and Australia.

It is clear that the use of ISO ILL in its current form is in decline. ISO ILL is based on lower-level constructs, such as ASN.1 and BER (Basic Encoding Rules), which were appropriate Open Systems Interconnection (OSI) protocol stacks common at the time of its initial development, but are not consistent with current technologies based on Internet technologies. ISO ILL has proven to be difficult to implement, requiring tedious testing and validation with each system that intends to exchange messages. Many of the systems that previously supported the protocol have since dropped its use. Docline, the document delivery service of the U.S. National Library of Medicine, dropped use of ISO ILL in January 2007.[3]

OCLC documents its support of ISO ILL, including its Protocol Implementation Conformance Statement.[4] OCLC provides a listing of libraries that have been profiled to use ISO ILL, which include only a handful of U.S. libraries that use FDX or had previously used RLG. A large number of libraries in Japan, affiliated through the National Institute of Informatics (NII), have also been profiled to submit requests to WorldCat Resource Sharing via the ISO ILL protocol. In the March 2012 meeting of the NCC ILL/DD Committee, it was mentioned that OCLC will phase out the use of the ISO ILL protocol.[5]

Activity is underway to redevelop the ISO ILL standard. At the Berlin ISO meeting in May 2012, ISO ILL Version 2 was ratified for an additional five years, and the decision was made that some minor editorial corrections would be implemented by Library and Archives Canada. More important, it was also recommended that a new international standard be drafted. An ad hoc group, including national representation from Australia, Canada, Denmark, Finland, Germany, Japan, New Zealand, the United Kingdom, and NISO, as well as the British Library and members from the infrastructure committee of the Rethinking Resource Sharing initiative, is working on drafting and putting forward a proposal for a new ISO ILL protocol. As opposed to the complex and fragile nature of the current ISO ILL, the new protocol is intended to be as simple as possible and based on current stateless web services technologies in order to foster wide implementation. The Danish National Library led the work to prepare ISO 10151–1:2014, published on November 1, 2014.[6]

APPLICATION PROGRAMMING INTERFACES

One of the general trends seen recently in the resource-sharing arena, consistent with other areas of library technology, involves the increased emphasis on application programming interfaces (APIs) implemented as RESTful (REpresentational State Transfer) web services. OCLC, for example, has developed a set of APIs for WorldShare Interlibrary Loan that provides much of the same capabilities as the ISO ILL protocol and that can be implemented with far less complexity. Many third-party applications, such as ILLiad, use this API to transfer requests and exchange messages with WorldCat Resource Sharing.

OPENURL REQUEST TRANSFER MESSAGE

Another approach that has been developed in this arena builds on the OpenURL protocol. Designed to transfer messages from discovery systems to fulfillment services, the Request Transfer Message encodes messages in similar form to the ISO ILL protocol as an XML document and encoded within the OpenURL syntax. Request Transfer Message has been defined as an OpenURL community profile, which defines the messages and data elements supported. The Request Transfer Message will include metadata describing the various entities involved. Mandatory elements include the Referent, or the item of interest; the Requestor; and the type of service requested. Optional elements include the referrer that generated the request; the referring entity, such as the article that contains the citation of the item of interest; and the base URL of the resolver. Detailed information describing all the elements of the OpenURL Request Transfer Message is available on the NISO website.

NISO CIRCULATION INTERCHANGE PROTOCOL (NCIP)

The automation of resource-sharing activities often involves interactions with the circulation module of an integrated library system. Direct consortial borrowing systems, for example, may need to perform a set of transactions to allow a patron from one partner library to place a request for an item held by another and for the libraries to use the functionality of their respective ILS circulation modules to manage the fulfillment of the request. The NISO Circulation Interchange Protocol, or NCIP, provides a set of procedures related to patron and item records in an ILS and the ability to perform operations related to circulation. The NCIP standard was initially published in 2002.

3M Library Systems, a major developer of self-service circulation equipment, developed the Standard Interchange Protocol, or SIP. This protocol includes directives related to patron and item records of an ILS and allows an external system, such as a self-check station, to perform circulation-related transactions. SIP was originally published in 1993, with a second version adopted in 2006. Version 3 of the protocol was developed in 2011. The SIP protocol was originally proposed by 3M and developed in conjunction with other related organizations, especially those involved with developing integrated library systems or self-service hardware and software. Although owned by 3M, SIP has been very widely implemented. In June 2012, 3M transferred ownership of the SIP protocol to NISO.[7]

SIP2 has been widely implemented, finding support in almost all of the major integrated library systems. Most of the ILS providers charge a separate license fee for their SIP module. Although NCIP includes similar capabilities, it has not been widely used in the library self-service arena.

Z39.50

Z39.50 was created as the international search-and-retrieval standard for bibliographic systems, primarily those based on MARC records. SRU (Search and Retrieve via URL) provides most of the capabilities of Z39.50 using current web-based protocols rather than the older ASN.1 and BER constructs. This protocol is very widely implemented with almost all integrated library systems offering a Z39.50 service, usually as an optional module.

Many resource-sharing environments include a discovery component to allow patrons to search a body of available resources. One of the techniques used to provide this discovery capability creates a virtual union catalog by dynamically searching multiple bibliographic sources. A direct consortial borrowing system, for example, might involve a virtual union catalog based on the catalog data available in the ILS of each participating library. Virtual union catalogs as part of resource-sharing systems generally rely on Z39.50 as their underlying search-and-retrieval protocol. Z39.50 is also used to retrieve bibliographic or holdings data in support of individual record displays involved in resource requests.

RETHINKING RESOURCE SHARING

The Rethinking Resource Sharing initiative was formed out of a group of individuals and organizations interested in making substantial improvements in this area of library service. The initiative developed white papers on relevant topics and produced a manifesto that asserted key values related to the ways that libraries make their resources available beyond their immediate clientele.

PRINCIPLES IN THE "MANIFESTO FOR RETHINKING RESOURCE SHARING"

- *Restrictions shall only be imposed as necessary* by individual institutions with the goal that the lowest-possible-barriers-to-fulfillment are presented to the user.

- *Library users shall be given appropriate options* for delivery format, method of delivery, and fulfillment type, including loan, copy, digital copy, and purchase.

- *Global access to sharable resources shall be encouraged* through formal and informal networking agreements with the goal towards lowest-barrier-to-fulfillment.

- *Sharable resources shall include those held in cultural institutions of all sorts:* libraries, archives, museums, and the expertise of those employed in such places.

- *Reference services are a vital component* to resource sharing and delivery and shall be made readily accessible from any initial "can't supply this" response. No material that is findable should be totally unattainable.

- *Libraries should offer service at a fair price* rather than refuse but should strive to achieve services that are not more expensive than commercial services, e.g., bookshops.

- *Library registration should be as easy as signing up for commercial web-based services.* Everyone can be a library user.

(From Rethinking Resource Sharing, "A Manifesto for Rethinking Resource Sharing," accessed October 17, 2012, http://rethinkingresourcesharing.org/manifesto.html)

The group's "Manifesto for Rethinking Resource Sharing" asserts the values listed in the sidebar.

The Rethinking Resource Sharing initiative organized committees related to user needs, policies, marketing, delivery, and infrastructure. The basic charge of the Infrastructure Committee was "to identify the technology framework that makes it possible for users to obtain what they find inside the library or outside on the open Web."[8] In addition to developing an environmental scan of the protocols and standards related to interlibrary loan, the committee launched the GoGetter project, to develop a modular plug-in for web browsers that would present a GetIt button to easily enable an individual to make a request for any item encountered on the Web.[9]

NOTES

1. Mary Jackson, "Overview of North American Interlibrary Loan Protocol Activities" (paper presented at the 63rd IFLA General Conference, Copenhagen, Denmark, August 31–September 5, 1997), http://archive.ifla.org/IV/ifla63/63jacm.htm.
2. Library and Archives Canada, "ISO ILL Protocol Standards: ISO 10160," Interlibrary Loan Application Standards Maintenance Agency, 1997, www.collectioscanada.gc.ca/iso/ill/stan160.htm.
3. U.S. National Library of Medicine, "Question: Does DOCLINE Support the ISO ILL Protocol?" FAQs, February 7, 2007, last updated July 13, 2012, www.nlm.nih.gov/services/doc_nlm_support_iso.html.
4. OCLC, "ISO ILL: The International Standard for Interlibrary Loan," www.oclc.org/isoill.
5. North American Coordinating Council on Japanese Library Resources, "NCC ILL/DD Committee Meeting in Hawaii" (meeting minutes, March 14, 2012), www.nccjapan.net/illdd/documents/ILLDDMinutes2012.pdf.
6. Clare McKeigan and Ed Davidson, "The Future of ILL Interoperability" (presentation at the 10th Nordic Resource Sharing, Reference and Collection Management Conference, Reykjavik, Iceland, October 3–5, 2012).
7. NISO, "Standard Interchange Protocol," www.niso.org/workrooms/sip.
8. Rethinking Resource Sharing, Interoperability Committee goals, http://rethinkingresourcesharing.org/charter.html.
9. Melissa Stockton, "Rethinking Resource Sharing Initiative" (presentation at the Moving Mountains Symposium, Denver, CO, September 25–26, 2008).

5

Types of Cloud Computing Solutions

I n this chapter we will move beyond the hype associated with cloud computing and take a detailed look at the range of major options for technology infrastructure. We begin by reviewing the characteristics of local computing in order to provide points of comparison with the domain of cloud computing and its many flavors. We then look at some of the hosting arrangements that begin to take libraries away from the realm of local control of computing, finally arriving at the services that more properly reside in the realm of cloud computing.

Today the term *cloud computing* pervades all aspects of discourse about technology, from the scholarly and professional press, to conference presentations, and especially to the promotional materials for products and services. It's become a buzzword and marketing tag loosely applied to a wide range of technical implementation and deployment arrangements. Many different products tend to be promoted through such catchphrases as "in the cloud" without necessarily clarifying the exact technical infrastructure involved. Some of these claims turn out to be more cloud-like than others.

An earlier version of this chapter was published in *Cloud Computing for Libraries* (The Tech Set #11).

This chapter will step through the various models of computing that tend to be classified as cloud computing either by formal or informal criteria. We will look at some of the broad characteristics encompassed within the realm of cloud computing and the major deployment options. Armed with this information, one can better evaluate the different technology options regardless of the marketing language used to promote specific products and services.

How an organization implements its computing environment can be thought of as a set of implementation options that vary across a spectrum of abstraction. At one end of that spectrum is the traditional model of local computing where one can see and touch all the components involved. At the other extreme are the most abstract models, such as software-as-a-service or platform-as-a-service. In between we see many different alternatives. While there are many different flavors of computing meant by "in the cloud," none of them relates to the tangible equipment that you can see and touch, but all involve some kind of remote or abstract service.

CONSIDER LOCAL DEPARTMENTAL COMPUTING

First, consider the computing model with the characteristics that form the strongest contrast to cloud computing. If your library maintains some or all of its servers that support its automation systems within its own building, it can be thought of as following the model of departmental computing. Many libraries may have a modest data center that houses all of its information technology equipment, including servers, storage arrays, routers, and network switches. This is a style of computing that you can see and touch, where the library has full ownership, control, and responsibility for the infrastructure from the ground up.

This infrastructure isn't necessarily just the computers themselves. Such a data center would also house lots of support equipment, such as individual uninterruptible power supplies for each server, or have a larger enterprise-class UPS to support all the equipment. Because computers produce so much heat, special cooling equipment will be needed to maintain reasonable operating temperatures. In many cases the cost of power and cooling equipment can represent as much of an investment as the computing equipment, and the ongoing costs in terms of increased utility bills can't be absent from cost calculations.

Some smaller libraries may have one or two servers that may reside in an office environment, such as in a systems department, and have more modest facilities overhead, but they may likewise not gain the benefits that server-class equipment really need for nonstop reliability and speedy performance. Midsized or larger libraries are more likely to purchase rack-mount computers that take less space, can be more easily managed, and are housed in data closets or a library computer room with more robust environmental controls. In addition to the physical facilities, the equipment housed in a departmental computer closet or data center requires the attention of technical personnel. Computer technicians, server administrators, or other trained personnel will be involved to install, configure, and maintain this equipment and to deal with problems as they happen.

Departmental computing offers several advantages. If the data center resides within the library, outages of the Internet connection or problems on the broader organization's network may not impact access between staff workstations and the integrated library system (ILS), leaving critical business functions such as circulation and online catalog functions intact. This arrangement also gives the library the highest degree of control in the way that applications are implemented and in priorities of service. When a problem occurs, the library's own staff can take remedial action without having to wait on institutional or external personnel to respond.

On the other hand, the model of departmental computing imposes the highest level of responsibility on the library and the highest cost. The library must absorb the full cost of purchasing the equipment, maintaining a suitable operating environment, and providing the requisite personnel resources. Equipment needs to be replaced every few years, resulting in an endless cycle of procurement, installation, and maintenance. The library's own personnel need to be on call at all times to deal with any interruptions in service that would have a negative impact on the operations of the library. These high thresholds of investment and cost have been key drivers in exploring alternatives to this approach to library computing in favor of other more enterprise-oriented and ultimately cloud-based models.

INVESTIGATE DIFFERENT HOSTING OPTIONS

Remote Website Hosting

Many libraries rely on institutional or commercial hosting services for their websites. In this case, the library isn't leasing an entire server but running its website through a hosting service. The library does not have to get involved with the hardware that supports the site but will contract for the service based on the number of pages involved, the bandwidth consumed, or other usage-based factors. Such a service might simply host pages as developed by the library, but many will provide consulting and design services and other assistance needed to create a professional presentation and organizational structure.

It's common for a library's web presence to be provided not directly by the library itself but by its parent organization. Especially in a university setting, the library might participate in an enterprise content management system rather than operate its own web server.

Some of the considerations of using an external website hosting service include the library's ability to run different kinds of scripting languages that might be needed for special features, support of content management systems such as Drupal or Joomla, and whether the library is able to directly access the files of the site to perform updates.

The operation of a library's website falls into the realm of the many aspects of technology in transition from complete local ownership and control toward enterprise-oriented or more abstract provision of its underlying infrastructure.

SERVER COLOCATION

Given the high costs of maintaining their own departmental computing facilities, many libraries enter arrangements to outsource the physical housing of their server infrastructure with some external provider. Libraries within larger organizations, such as colleges, universities, research facilities, medical centers, hospitals, corporations, municipal or county governments, and the like may be able to take advantage of larger-scale, consolidated data centers that provide technical infrastructure for all their units or departments in addition to the infrastructure they maintain on behalf of the organization as a whole. The movement from departmental to enterprise computing has been one of the major information technology trends of the past two decades. Having each department within an organization house its own computing infrastructure is much less efficient than relying on more sophisticated and robust, industrial-strength services for the entire organization. Having one centralized e-mail service for the whole organization, for example, offers far more efficiency than multiple departmental servers. An enterprise data center will operate applications such as finance, payroll, e-mail, or other communications services that benefit the entire organization. In addition, most of these data centers house, and at least partially operate, specialized servers and services on behalf of units and departments throughout the organization. In this vein, campus data centers routinely house the servers for a library's automation system.

In most colocation arrangements, the library would continue to have ownership and some degree of responsibility for the server. A typical arrangement might involve the central IT staff taking responsibility for physical hardware maintenance and operating system issues, with the library assuming responsibility for software applications, such as the ILS, digital asset management environment, or other library-specific applications.

It is also possible for libraries to take advantage of colocation arrangements with external commercial providers. Libraries that don't want to house their own servers but are not part of a larger organization can contract with external hosting companies to house their equipment in industrial-strength data centers.

Server colocation represents the first step away from local computing to more abstract approaches. It essentially outsources the housing and upkeep of the hardware to an external entity. Although the hardware is "out of sight," it is not "out of mind," however, because it continues to require technical management by the library.

DEDICATED SERVER HOSTING

A similar approach involves contracting for the use of a server from an institutional or commercial data center. In this arrangement, the data center owns the equipment and provides exclusive use of it for a set price per month or year. Dedicated server hosting eliminates the up-front costs of purchasing the hardware. The customer, such as a library contracting for a server to host its ILS, retains full control over the administration of the operating system and applications. The cost of a dedicated server may also vary according to the operating system provided. It is more expensive, for example, to contract for a server running a commercial operating system such as Microsoft Windows Server, where the license fees must be amortized, than for open source options such as Linux.

In a dedicated server hosting environment, the library has exclusive control of the server equipment. Only applications installed by the library will run on it, possibly with the exception of management modules that the hosting facility might want to install to ensure its optimal operation. Access to the server for administration would be accomplished through tools such as a secure shell for Linux- or Unix-based systems or through Remote Desktop or Remotely Anywhere for Windows servers.

From an operational perspective, a dedicated server hosting arrangement resembles colocation arrangements. The key difference is the business model whereby colocation involves equipment owned by the customer and dedicated hosting essentially leases servers provided by the provider. Dedicated hosting tends to involve external commercial providers rather than institutional data centers.

In a dedicated hosting arrangement, end-user access to the application travels through the provider's Internet connectivity rather than the library's.

In most cases this arrangement results in much higher bandwidth capacity to the server than would be the case if this traffic passed through the library's network. Because access by library personnel passes through the Internet instead of the local network, some concerns may apply to the security of the connections, which can be resolved through the use of a VPN (virtual private network).

Dedicated hosting makes sense when the library needs full control of the server and a highly reliable environment. A commercial hosting company can offer a more secure environment with many layers of redundancy for power, cooling, and Internet connectivity than a library would be able to provide within its own facilities. Dedicated hosting may be a reasonable alternative for custom-developed applications or for proprietary or open source products not offered through software-as-a-service, as described later.

VIRTUAL SERVER HOSTING

Moving toward more abstract models of computing, a library may be able to run its applications on a virtualized server rather than a dedicated server. In this case, the library gains access to an instance of an operating environment that may coexist on a server with other instances. In other words, the library gets access to a full running version of an operating environment but does not gain exclusive access to the hardware upon which it runs.

Virtual hosting can be considerably less expensive than dedicated server hosting. Because the provider can let out multiple virtual servers for each physical server, its overhead is substantially lower. To take advantage of the lower costs of virtual server hosting over a dedicated server, the applications involved must be well-tested for a virtualized environment, and the processing required should be below the threshold that requires a dedicated server to satisfy.

Both virtual server hosting and dedicated server hosting tend to be priced at a fixed rate per month or per year and not variable according to use levels, as we will see later for the offerings more properly associated with cloud computing.

MOVE INTO THE REALM OF CLOUD COMPUTING

Infrastructure as a Service

As we consider the differing models of computer infrastructure deployment, infrastructure-as-a-service, often abbreviated IaaS, falls within what would more legitimately be considered cloud computing. This model breaks away from thinking of computing in terms of specific servers toward a more flexible and abstract approach to gaining the right level of capacity for an organization's technical infrastructure.

IaaS involves subscribing to computing and storage capabilities on an as-needed basis. This model differs from the dedicated or virtual server hosting models in that the allocation and pricing of the computing resources vary by actual consumption rather than fixed monthly fees. IaaS allows an organization to gain access to computing resources—such as an instance of Linux or Windows—scaled to the demands and duration of a project. A short-term development task, for example, can be accomplished at minimal cost. The environment of major production systems can be built on IaaS, deployed on computing resources appropriately scaled in terms of number of processors, memory available per processor, disk storage capacity and services such as geographic replication, or disaster recovery options.

With IaaS, the organization will never see the physical hardware involved, but will perform much of the systems administration tasks as they would for local servers. Operating an application through IaaS saves the organization from the purchase of its own hardware, eliminates the overhead associated with the maintenance of hardware, but retains the tasks associated with installing and maintaining software applications.

Resources allocated to an application can be increased and decreased according to anticipated use. This "elastic" characteristic of IaaS ensures adequate capacity during peak periods with the ability to step down allocated resources should use levels fall. When an organization delivers an application through IaaS, it pays for only the computing resources it uses, with much more flexibility than would apply to locally owned equipment or dedicated or virtual hosting arrangements.

IaaS can be deployed for many different kinds of scenarios: a development and production environment for custom-developed software, a platform for implementing licensed commercial software, or open source applications. A library might use IaaS to operate its ILS, for example, rather than purchase local hardware. An ILS vendor might use IaaS as the infrastructure to support its software-as-a-service or application service provider offerings.

Exploration or implementation of infrastructure services can be phased in gradually. Organizations that base their computing environment on local computing equipment might consider implementing some aspect of supplemental resources through IaaS. Projects involving custom software, development, prototypes, and testing can take place on resources allocated through IaaS even when the production environment will run on dedicated servers. A development environment can be ramped up and torn down as needed, providing a very inexpensive and flexible way to support a library's research and development efforts. Copies of data, programming code, and configuration files can reside on more persistent storage allocations, even when computing resources have been set aside. This approach provides a flexible way for programmers to have access to computing resources, without having to deal with all the technical and procedural overhead involved in procuring, installing, and maintaining local hardware. Although there are many other providers, Amazon.com ranks as one of the most popular providers of IaaS. It's Elastic Compute Cloud, or EC2, service provides access to either Windows or Linux computing instances delivered through Amazon Machine Images. When procuring this service, the customer specifies such things as whether to use Windows or Linux as the operating system and to select from a range of memory and processor options, with prices per hour scaled accordingly.

DATA STORAGE IN THE CLOUD

In the current environment, devices and equipment for storing data have become incredibly inexpensive and flexible. USB-attached disk drives with capacities of up to 3 TB are now available for today for little more than $100, and 16 GB flash drives can be purchased for less than $10. Given the incredible amounts of storage available at such little cost, is there a need for storage delivered through the cloud?

Although storage options based on tangible local devices may be inexpensive and flexible in lots of ways, they also have disadvantages. USB flash drives can easily be misplaced and are inherently insecure. Few users of these devices bother to perform file encryption or employ other techniques to prevent anyone who comes across a misplaced device from accessing files. Misplacing one of these devices can result in a sensitive file leaking beyond its intended audience or not having a copy of your presentation files when you need them for an important speech.

Keep in mind the inherent fragility of all physical storage devices. They can fail at any time and can be lost or destroyed by unforeseen events. The data on the internal drive in your laptop or desktop computer can be lost through hardware failures, software malfunctions, malware attacks, or through human error. It's essential to have many copies of any computer file of importance.

The utmost care needs to be given to both personal and organizational data. Anyone would feel devastated to lose personal files such as family photos, financial information, genealogy research, or other kinds of information that represented untold hours of work to create. Most individuals and organizations think about and plan for what physical items might be lost in a fire, flood, burglary, or other major incident. It's also important to think about our digital assets. If all the computing equipment in your home were stolen or destroyed, would you be able to recover all your files from copies stored elsewhere? One of the basic strategies for data security involves keeping multiple copies spread across multiple geographic locations. Having all the copies of digital assets in your home doesn't offer adequate protection. Keeping an extra copy at your office or at a friend's or relative's place is better; having a copy in a distant city is even better.

Placing copies of data on physical devices stored in different geographic locations can be an inconvenient process, especially when it comes to keeping all the copies up-to-date. Every time you add a batch of new photos, for example, you would need to find a way to get copies onto the drives you have in remote locations. Cloud-based storage can be used to address the vulnerabilities inherent in relying solely on physical devices for important digital assets.

IaaS involves storing files and data through an external provider. Cloud-based storage, sometimes called storage-as-a-service, represents a major component of IaaS. These services accommodate many different types of use, ranging from casual personal use to large-scale mission-critical enterprise implementations. Storage services can be used in association with full-blown applications deployed through IaaS, as a backup mechanism for locally hosted applications, as a means to transfer data from one individual or organization to another, or as a temporary work space for a project. Just about any activity that involves either short-term or long-term storage of data can take advantage of storage delivered through the cloud for flexible access and often with less expense than purchasing local storage.

Amazon's Simple Storage Service, or S3, provides disk storage through a web service. The configuration of the storage, involving factors such as the level of redundancy and backup services provided, will impact the unit costs and expected reliability and disaster recovery possibilities. Data related to mission-critical services can be allocated storage with more redundancy and services than would be needed for temporary storage of data where primary copies exist elsewhere. Environments based on EC2 will likely use S3 for storage of data and program files. It's also very common to use S3 independently for projects that benefit from cloud-based storage but are accessed in other ways. S3, while protecting data as private by default, can also be configured to share files either to other users of the Amazon Web Services or as widely as needed through enabling access by publishing them to the Web.

ADDRESSING THE NEED
FOR PERSONAL PORTABLE STORAGE

Many data storage services are geared toward personal users, offering modest amounts of space at little or no cost. These services provide a very convenient way for individuals to have portable access to their files and to share data with others. These are a few such services:

Dropbox (www.dropbox.com) offers a free 2 GB storage option, with installable client drivers that make the service appear as any other folder. Dragging files into the folder automatically initiates transfer to Dropbox, which can then be shared with other users. Dropbox is a convenient way for an individual to share files among multiple computers (Windows, Mac, Linux) and mobile devices (iPhone, iPad, Android, BlackBerry).

Google Drive (https://www.google.com/drive) offers 15 GB of free storage to every Google account holder. That allotment is shared with whatever storage your Gmail account uses. You can upload all file types. You can use the Google apps software suite to create or edit files.

Microsoft One-Drive (https://onedrive.live.com/about/en-us) offers free storage up to 5 GB. Built in to Windows 8 and 10 operating systems, it works across all the common platforms, with versions for Mac OS, iOS, Android, and Xbox apps. It will store any file type—videos, photos, or document. OneDrive's strength is its integration into Microsoft Windows and the Office suite of business applications. Once uploaded to OneDrive, documents can be edited directly on Microsoft's web-based Office 365 applications or with Office applications installed on a user's workstation. OneDrive can be used as a backup copy as a contingency against problems with those stored on a hard drive of a laptop or desktop computer. As with other cloud storage services, documents stored on OneDrive are available only when the user is connected to the Internet. This limitation requires users to rely on local documents when connectivity is not available.

Amazon Cloud Drive (https://www.amazon.com/clouddrive/learnmore) offers its Amazon Prime members limited free storage plans. It also offers a couple of fee-based subscription plans: one for photos only and another for all file types.

Box.net (www.box.net) is a cloud storage provider mostly oriented to businesses.

ADrive (www.adrive.com) offers large allotments of storage at relatively low rates, supported by third-party advertisements. The personal plan offers 100 GB for a few dollars per month.

Cloud storage services provide a very convenient way to deal with all of the files and data that pervade our personal and work lives. For personal files, free storage services allow one to have multiple copies of files to reduce the odds of losing important information, usually the products of hours of work. Given the current abundance of free services, it would be a good strategy to make copies of files on one or two cloud storage services in addition to the copies held on a laptop or desktop computer.

Cloud storage services can also be used for work-related files, but it's important to be sure that this use is consistent with the expectations of your employer. Most libraries provide shared drives on file servers where they expect personnel to store their documents. These shared network drives can be configured to provide shared access to the teams, work groups, or committees to facilitate collaboration. If individuals within these teams instead place their files on a separate cloud-based service, it may disrupt the processes and procedures established for the organization. If these kinds of services are not provided in the work environment, then cloud services may be an approach to consider for establishing them.

But it's important to be aware of their limitations as well as their benefits—one should not become overly reliant on any given service. You cannot expect a free service to take any responsibility for your data. If you lose your user name or password, accidently delete files, or lose data through any other kind of technical mishap, you cannot expect the service to recover the account or restore your files. These are the kinds of features offered with the paid premium services of the cloud storage providers. Likewise, even if the loss is due to a failure of the provider, the provider may not be under any obligation to protect or restore your files. Most importantly, be prepared for the service to go out of business or for the withdrawal of free services in favor of paid accounts. Although it seems likely that free services will continue to prosper, they should be treated as a convenience, not as the sole basis for preserving important assets.

Given the importance of protecting individual or institutional data, it's essential to implement a strategy that delivers an adequate level of protection. Such a strategy might include a combination of local and cloud-based storage, synchronizing copies across multiple independent cloud services, or subscribing to cloud services with multiple layers of disaster recovery services. For institutional data, be sure to consult and collaborate with the organization's IT department to ensure that your use of cloud services complements and does not contradict their efforts to ensure efficient, reliable, and secure treatment of your organization's data assets.

SOFTWARE-AS-A-SERVICE

One of the most popular forms of cloud computing today involves the access to software applications over the Web rather than using individual instances installed on a local workstation or provided through an organization's servers. This model of computing provides access to all features and functionality of an application without having to be involved in the technical details of how it is hosted. In its purest form, users access the application through a web browser, with all the data involved stored on the provider's servers.

Applications delivered through the software-as-a-service (SaaS) model ideally follow a multi-tenant architecture. This characteristic involves the ability for a single instance of the application to be shared among many different organizations or individual users simultaneously. All users of the software might be able to configure the software for their specific needs, and their data will be partitioned appropriately. Whether the SaaS application is geared toward organizations or individual users, layers of authentication and authorization in conjunction with appropriate data architectures ensure that each tenant of the application gains access to its full functionality with complete assurance that others will not gain unauthorized access to their data. SaaS can also be used in collaborative ways when users explicitly elect to share data. SaaS offers a much more efficient approach relative to traditional locally installed software both for the provider and for the consumer. These efficiencies have driven the software industry toward this deployment model, although many legacy applications remain—especially in the library automation arena.

From the provider's perspective, there is just one instance of the software to support, operating on a single platform. Enhancements and bug fixes can be implemented once for all customers. While the scale of the platform comes with its own challenges and complications, much smaller levels of effort are needed to support each organization or individual customer. With traditional software, whether hosted by the vendor in an application service provider arrangement or on the customer's premises, upgrades must be installed for each of these separate instances. The complexity increases as different customer sites may operate the software on different brands and configurations of hardware, under different operating systems, and even with local customizations that confound routine upgrade and support issues.

From the consumer's perspective, SaaS eliminates multiple layers of technical support, because it requires no local server hardware, no software installed on each end-user computer, and no technical administration of operating systems, database engines, or other infrastructure components. SaaS shifts much of the responsibility for maintaining an application from the organization to the provider. Version updates, patches, enhancements, and other changes to the software appear automatically rather than having to be installed by the customer. The traditional software deployment model, because of the great effort involved, often results in libraries operating software that is years out of date and thus not being able to access current features, bug fixes, and security patches.

One of the classic examples of an SaaS targeting organizational implementations is Salesforce.com (www.salesforce.com), a customer relationship management (CRM) platform used by many tens of thousands of companies and other organizations worldwide to manage their sales and support activities. It stands as the epitome of cloud computing. Organizations that subscribe to Salesforce.com create a customized environment that provides a comprehensive environment for tracking customers, automates the sales process, and offers a dashboard of metrics and analytics that measure the performance of the company in each of its activities. Salesforce.com also offers its own platform-as-a-service, Force.com (http://force.com), that organizations can use to build their own custom applications.

The library automation arena continues to be dominated by traditional software designed to be implemented for individual libraries or consortia. Only some of the more recent products have been designed and deployed through SaaS. Serials Solutions, now part of Ex Libris, a ProQuest Company, for example, was one of the early companies in the library arena to offer its products exclusively in an SaaS model, including its 360 Suite of products for management and access to electronic resources and its Summon discovery service. Many of the new generation of library automation products are being designed for SaaS, including Primo Central and Alma from Ex Libris, and WorldShare Management Services and WorldCat Discovery Service from OCLC and EBSCO Discovery Service. Yet the majority of the library automation products available today were created prior to the time when cloud computing concepts such as multi-tenant SaaS entered the technology scene. See chapter 6 for a more detailed treatment of the library automation products and services based on cloud technologies.

The payment model for SaaS varies depending on many factors, including whether it is intended for personal or institutional use. Commercial business applications, such as major library automation systems, would be made available through a monthly or annual subscription fee. The terms of a subscription to an SaaS offering would specify such things as what customer support will be provided, guaranteed availability, and other details. The cost of the subscription will be set according to consumption factors, such as modules or options deployed, numbers of monthly transactions, or as monthly or annual charges based on the size and complexity of the organization or the potential number of users in the organization.

Many of the most popular productivity or communications applications, either in the context of personal or business use, are accessed through SaaS. Obvious examples include Gmail and Google Docs. Users consume these applications through their web browsers, with no local software.

An increasing number of applications originally offered as locally installed software are transitioning to SaaS or other cloud-based delivery models. Examples include Microsoft's Office 365, a cloud-based SaaS, mentioned earlier, that provides similar functionality to the Office suite of productivity applications designed to be installed on individual computers. In the personal and small business finance realm, products such as Intuit's QuickBooks have evolved from software installed on individual computers to also being offered as web-based services, as has its TurboTax tax preparation software.

Organizations involved in creating products offered through an SaaS often depend on other providers to host their applications. It's possible, or even likely, that a company offering a library automation system through SaaS will deploy the software using computing resources through an IaaS provider such as Amazon.com, provisioning the requisite number of server images and storage through EC2 and S3, or might contract with a major server-hosting facility such as Rackspace or Equinix. Organizations with core expertise in software development and support are not necessarily the ones best positioned to deliver highly reliable infrastructure services.

APPLICATION SERVICE PROVIDER

The concept of using software applications via the Internet is not especially recent, with many software firms offering their products in hosted arrangements since the 1990s through an arrangement called "application service provider," or ASP. This deployment model relies on the server component of a business application to be hosted by a vendor—usually the company that developed the software—rather than at the customer's site. In the era of client/server computing, the standard configuration consisted of the server component installed in the data center of an organization, accessed by graphical clients installed on the computers of end users. In the context of an ILS, for example, the library operates the server component, with specialized Windows, Macintosh, or Java clients installed on the workstations of any personnel who operate the system. Library users access the public catalog of the system through a web browser. The traditional client/server application includes a server component installed in the library, specialized clients for library personnel, and web-based online catalog for library patrons; each instance of the server application supports a single library or consortium.

In the ASP arrangement, all aspects of the client/server deployment remain the same, but the server component resides in a data center operated by the software provider and the clients access that server through the Internet instead of the local network. The provider maintains individual instances of the server component that correspond to each library or consortium making use of the product.

This model of software deployment provides many of the characteristics of SaaS for legacy applications not specifically designed for multi-tenant access. It offers significant benefits for libraries, or other organizations, taking advantage of the service, though it imposes higher thresholds of effort for the providers of the service.

From the perspective of the library, most of the benefits of SaaS apply, such as relief from the maintenance of local hardware and the technical details of administering the operating system and software applications, as well as the budget model of fixed subscription pricing rather than variable local technical and personnel expenses. This model does not provide relief in dealing with the specialized clients associated with the applications. In the context

TABLE 5.1

Features of the Software-as-a-Service and
Application Service Provider Models

Multi-Tenant SaaS	Application Service Provider
One instance serves all organizational or individual users	One instance per organization
All functionality delivered through web-based interfaces	Specialized clients (Windows, Mac, Java)
Data managed by provider	Data managed by provider
Access to application via Internet	Access to application via Internet
Provider administers software and deploys new versions	Provider administers software and deploys new versions
Consumption-based pricing or set subscription fees	Set subscription fees
Service access through the Internet	Service access through the Internet

of the ILS, the graphical clients continue to need to be installed on each staff workstation, replete with the requirement to install upgrades and maintain the configuration details for each workstation. The option to deploy through ASP naturally depends on the library having sufficient Internet bandwidth to support the traffic between the staff and end-user clients and the vendor-hosted server.

From the perspective of the vendor, the ASP model requires much more effort than would a multi-tenant SaaS environment. The vendor must maintain individual instances of the server application for each customer site, including all configuration selections, policy parameters, database tables, and other complexities. Through virtualization and other techniques that allow for large-scale consolidation of computing resources, an ASP can achieve much greater efficiencies than would apply to individual installations at customer sites, though still falling short of the full benefits of multi-tenant SaaS. Table 5.1 compares the SaaS and ASP models.

It is common for products delivered through what might more correctly be considered ASP to be marketed as SaaS. It is reasonable to consider ASP as a subset of the broader concept of SaaS, but a library should be well-informed regarding the issues described in this section.

PLATFORM AS A SERVICE

Organizations that create custom applications can take advantage of a platform-as-a-service (PaaS), which offers a complete development and production environment, abstracted from concerns with details of underlying infrastructure. Such a platform would offer a complete technology stack, including support for a programming language or applications programming interface, database functionality, data stores, computational resources, and other components needed to create a complete web-based application. A platform will provide a software development kit, or SDK, to provide the documentation that programmers need to create applications. Some of the best-known PaaS offerings include the following:

Google App Engine (http://code.google.com/appengine) supports programming languages such as Java, Python, and Go (an open source programming language created by Google).

Amazon Web Services (http://aws.amazon.com) includes a complex set of products spanning both IaaS and PaaS.

Force.com (www.force.com) is the underlying platform for Salesforce.com that can be used to create custom applications, primarily through a web-based development environment.

Bungee Connect (www.bungeeconnect.com) is a platform for the development of cloud-based apps that will be deployed on IaaS such as Amazon's EC2.

Heroku (www.heroku.com) is a PaaS for the Ruby programming language, including both development and a fully managed deployment environment.

The realm of PaaS offerings is of interest primarily to individuals or organizations that develop web-based applications. This approach can also be used to create add-ons to existing applications. Many library developers, for example, have written utilities and extensions making use of OCLC's WorldShare Platform as a development platform. Building on top of a PaaS not only simplifies development by avoiding the need for programmers to deal with operating system and infrastructure issues, but also results in highly scalable and robust applications with inherent cloud-computing characteristics.

UNDERSTAND THE PROS AND CONS OF CLOUD COMPUTING

While cloud computing offers a method of computing with a number of advantages, it comes with issues and limitations that a library must take into consideration as it considers increased involvement. No technology can be expected to offer only positive traits. Any negative characteristics need to be understood up-front so that even if the balance leans toward adopting the technology the appropriate measures are taken to mitigate risk and maximize advantages.

SECURITY ISSUES

In general, concerns for security and privacy should be considered neutral when comparing cloud computing with local systems management. The same types of tools and techniques are available across both environments for ensuring tight security. The same lapses in security can take place under either approach. Through IaaS offerings, such as Amazon's EC2, libraries can be assured of working with the instances of operating systems replete with the latest security patches. One of the significant advantages of cloud services lies in the provider taking responsibility for software and operating system updates. These providers have a great deal at stake in avoiding the kinds of embarrassing issues that would arise from security breaches that might be caused through offering instances of virtual machines out of date or missing critical security patches.

Taking advantage of cloud services does not eliminate the responsibility for an organization to take reasonable security measures. Password management, proper use of encryption for passing sensitive information, policies against sharing authentication credentials, and other standard security policies and practices apply regardless of the deployment model implemented.

Any custom-developed applications will have basically the same security concerns when operated in an IaaS environment as they would on local hardware. Programmers must code with care to avoid vulnerabilities such as cross-site scripting, SQL injections, or any of the techniques that can be exploited without rigorous defensive measures.

Security concerns for applications accessed through SaaS will vary relative to the attention the provider pays to these issues. Given the higher stakes and likelihood that an organization offering an SaaS product to a large number of customers would have deep technical resources, including seasoned system administrators and security specialists, libraries should expect a lower level of risk than with local hosting and fewer technical specialists. When procuring major library applications through SaaS, expectations regarding security practices and privacy of data should be clearly understood and incorporated into the terms of the subscription agreement.

Libraries have responsibilities to safeguard the privacy of data. While much of the data that libraries manage is intended to be widely shared, such as the bibliographic databases that describe their collections, some categories must be well-guarded as private, such as personal details of library patrons, the library's personnel records, or certain financial information. It's essential that any cloud-based deployments that involve sensitive data follow the standard practices, such as using TLS 1.2 to deliver web communications via https for any log-in to accounts that provide access to sensitive data and to encrypt any web pages that present personal details. It is increasingly an expectation that all web pages related to a library discovery service or resource management system be transmitted via https. Organizations such as financial firms and military or government agencies that deal with classified information, trade secrets, or other highly sensitive data tend to avoid using public cloud implementations that might allow co-mingling of data on a physical infrastructure outside of their direct ownership or control. Such an organization would be more likely to use a local infrastructure or a private cloud environment that partitions an organization's data and computing resources away from that of other tenants.

From a privacy and security perspective, comfort levels for using cloud-based products vary depending on the type of information and activity involved. E-mail, because it involves messages that will be exposed to the Internet anyway, is not an application that causes much concern. Savvy e-mail users know not to send any messages that contain highly sensitive content or to use some kind of encryption as needed. General word-processing files, such as student papers, general office correspondence and reports, or professional work, likewise do not trigger a great deal of worry. Standard restrictions through authenticated accounts provide reasonable security and privacy. Personal or institutional financial information, however, tends to invoke a bit more concern. When choosing whether to shift from local applications to a cloud-based service, it's prudent to be sure that the organization is aware and informed and gives consistent attention to the use of externally provided computing resources with any categories of data that might be perceived as sensitive.

RELIABILITY ISSUES

Libraries, like most organizations, have a low tolerance for interruptions in service. We also tend to have a very high reliance on the integrity of data. The operational, bibliographic, and financial data held within an ILS represents untold hours of effort and would be catastrophic if lost; any interruptions in service can be extremely inconvenient to library patrons and personnel. The data related to a library's digital collection may be unique and irreplaceable. As with any technology option, cloud computing is vulnerable to failures.

While expected levels of reliability may be extremely high, responsible use of cloud computing for mission-critical applications demands a set of disaster recovery plans that would be followed for locally implemented projects.

Cloud-based services have been designed to offer a much higher level of reliability than most organizations can accomplish within their own data centers. Large-scale cloud providers such as Amazon, Google, and Rackspace base their services on an architecture designed to withstand failures. Well-designed cloud services assume that any hardware component will fail and that the requests will be rerouted accordingly with no perceptible interruption in service. The data centers themselves have multiple layers of power protection and other environmental controls to be less vulnerable to local events that affect the availability of electricity. Amazon, for example, offers options where a service may be supported through multiple geographically separated zones to support organizations that must deliver extremely fault-tolerant applications.

Although cloud computing generally delivers much higher levels of reliability than local hosting arrangements, failures do happen. The reputation for the reliability of cloud services became a bit tarnished on April 21, 2011, when Amazon Web Services experienced a major failure that resulted in outages for many products that rely on its infrastructure, including Foursquare, Reddit, Quora, and HootSuite. The outage lasted for the greater part of a day, and many applications experienced longer service interruptions depending on what was needed to restore their operations. This event highlighted that organizations must plan for failures, even when they depend on cloud-based infrastructure. Amazon's customers who took advantage of multi-region deployments, for example, were able to avoid the service interruption. It's not sufficient to just put your data and application on a cloud-based infrastructure and hope for the best. Cloud services such as Amazon's EC2 offer a wide range of deployment options, allowing organizations to design the appropriate level of contingency plans. In the same manner that one would implement routine data backup procedures for locally hosted applications, the same kinds of considerations apply for any cloud-based implementation. Infrastructure failures can still happen, though with less frequency; vulnerability to errant software events or human error doesn't magically disappear. Stringent data preservation and backup procedures must be designed into any use of cloud services, whether it's for personal use or for your organization.

Fortunately, it's fairly easy to implement backup and contingency plans with cloud services. Many services will offer backup services as an added-cost option. These services will include procedures similar to what an organization would perform for its local servers, such as regular backup copies made to alternate media, such as tape, with the ability to rapidly restore files in the event of failure of the cloud storage system or data corruption through problems with the customer's application software. But these services may significantly increase the storage costs. While raw cloud-based storage can appear on the surface to be quite inexpensive, it's essential to also factor in services for reasonable disaster recovery contingencies.

Another strategy for protecting your data is to place copies on other, separate cloud storage services with regular synchronizing. It's extremely unlikely that failures would take place simultaneously among separate, geographically dispersed storage services. If you rely on multiple storage services, be sure that they are actually separate and not resident on the same physical data centers. For projects involving a modest amount of data—measured in gigabytes rather than terabytes—strategies involving multiple storage services can be implemented with little expense. The cost of the storage, the bandwidth involved in moving it, or other safety measures may be well below the expense of the components involved for regular backups of locally managed data, such as disk-to-disk backup hardware, tape drives and media, and enterprise backup software.

For an additional measure of safety, libraries may also want to keep local copies of data for projects that involve cloud-based services. For an SaaS ILS deployment, for example, these copies can provide insurance against business failures or contract disputes as much as for technical failures.

For strategies involving duplicate copies of data on alternate cloud services or local storage, some type of automatic process should be implemented to ensure that the backup copies are recent enough to be helpful in the event of a failure. In most cases, scheduled scripts can be implemented to refresh the copies as frequently as needed. The tried-and-true concepts of file management should be applied regardless of the deployment model: full backups made weekly or monthly with daily or hourly incremental backups for changed or modified files.

Most SaaS arrangements for major applications include service-level agreements that specify what actions the provider will implement to protect data. The measures required should meet or exceed the standard practices that a library would follow for locally managed systems. Depending on the level of assurance provided in the service-level agreement and the confidence that the library has in the provider, additional measures may be instituted to receive local copies of data as an added level of protection.

Other cloud-oriented applications, such as e-mail services, may not warrant extensive measures beyond those bundled with the product. Some categories of data would be inconvenient to lose access to for a limited period but would not necessarily result in a major interruption of the library's services.

The library's Internet connectivity can also impact the perceived reliability of the cloud-based services on which it relies. If the library has unstable or inadequate bandwidth, it may not be able to connect to service from external providers, causing interruptions for library personnel and for users within the library, even when remote users can access the services without problems. Robust access to the Internet is one of the key prerequisites of involvement with cloud computing.

On the whole, cloud-based services can offer a much higher level of reliability than most libraries are able to accomplish on their own equipment. Few libraries have the capacity to purchase the hardware necessary to implement the levels of redundancy routinely implemented in major cloud service facilities.

LARGE-SCALE DATA

Some libraries deal with very large-scale sets of data, involving many terabytes or even petabytes of content. Large-scale video collections, scientific data sets, or large image collections are a few examples of the library projects that involve immense quantities of data storage.

It's clear that cloud-based services, such as Amazon's S3, can handle data on a very large scale. But there may be practical limitations that may make local storage a better choice. The cost advantages between local storage and cloud storage change dramatically with very large-scale data sets. The 140 TB of storage underlying the Vanderbilt Television News Archive, for example, would incur monthly charges of $4,928 , or $59,150 per year, or $295,704 over a five-year period, if stored in the Amazon S3 service. These numbers greatly exceed the costs for purchasing the equipment to provide equivalent storage capacity on the organization's local network. Such costs continue to decrease. The same 150 TB had a monthly charge of $16,560 in 2011.

Another factor in dealing with very large-scale storage involves the time and cost of the bandwidth required for a transfer from its local source to a storage provider. Most storage service providers include charges for incoming and outgoing transfers, though these costs are quite modest compared to storage. The time required for the transfer of very large files can also be prohibitive. While some major universities and research centers have access to very high bandwidth through Internet2, the majority of libraries have more modest connectivity, and routine transfers of large data sets could take hours or days. Recognizing how cumbersome it may be to transfer large amounts of data, Amazon offers a service whereby a customer can ship a physical drive and Amazon will upload its contents into an S3 bucket.

The positive and negative factors balance differently as projects scale up from those that manage mere gigabytes to those that involve dozens or hundreds of terabytes. The positive aspects of increased flexibility, convenient access, and reliability still apply, but the costs can skyrocket and logistical tasks to transfer into and out of the cloud storage services become more challenging. While there may be some cases where a library might find it expedient to use cloud storage for these kinds of projects, current pricing models and bandwidth capacities make it a less viable option.

ENVIRONMENTAL ISSUES

Cloud computing results in a reduced environmental impact through reduced amounts of energy consumed relative to the use of discrete equipment. The cumulative resources consumed by hundreds of servers, as might be operated in a typical university data center, or thousands or tens of thousands, as are routinely managed in commercial data centers, can make a major environmental impact. The consolidation of servers through virtualization, or through more aggressive computer utilization accomplished through cloud computing, results in fewer physical servers and proportional savings in energy consumption.

The use of cloud-based services will reduce consumption of energy resources within the library. Operating fewer servers results in an incremental reduction in power and cooling resources. Fully eliminating a library's data center will make an even more noticeable impact. Greater energy savings are gained through the consolidation of equipment from many smaller data centers to larger facilities with more efficient power utilization, at least on a per-server basis. Transferring servers from a smaller and less energy-efficient computer room in the library to an institutional data center or an external hosting center or cloud service not only reduces the library's energy bills but also energy consumption overall. Reducing power consumption by moving away from less efficient local servers to other less consumptive models can be seen as a positive contribution to an organization's green initiative.

VERSION CONTROL

When operating locally installed software, keeping applications up-to-date with current versions can be a major challenge. Planning for major software upgrades, or even minor patches, requires intervention of the library's technical personnel. Major functional upgrades that involve new or changed functionality in the way that library personnel use the software or that impacts end-user features may require significant training and testing. Many academic libraries, for example, interested in avoiding disruptions during busy periods, will schedule major updates to take place during breaks in the academic calendar. Major updates can also require higher levels of hardware support, which may exceed the capacity of the library's server equipment. Especially in the realm of ILSs, many libraries operate versions of the software that are many years out of date even when they are entitled to updates through their maintenance or support fees.

SaaS shifts the burden of implementing software updates from the library's local staff to the vendor. Although major updates may still require scheduling, minor updates and patches can be routinely implemented by the vendor across all the customers subscribing to the service. Major updates may require some coordination on scheduling. Because the SaaS provider takes responsibility for the hardware platform, the need to upgrade customer hardware does not apply as it does with local installations.

FLEXIBLE ENVIRONMENT FOR LIBRARY DEVELOPERS

An area where cloud computing really shines lies in the realm of software development. For libraries involved in the creation of custom applications or other tech-heavy projects, cloud-based services can provide many benefits.

Maintaining local computers for development involves considerable effort and expense. Local computers require ongoing cost commitments, from procurement, to maintenance, through replacement. Time investment in dealing with local hardware adds a layer of overhead that detracts from the essential tasks involved in software development. Purchasing and setting up a server for development can take days or weeks to prepare. Ramping up a server instance through an IaaS such as Amazon's EC2 can be done in a matter of minutes. This approach can facilitate the rapid creation of prototypes that, delivered through a cloud service, can be accessed and critiqued from anywhere on the Internet. Cloud-based development can be especially well-suited to distributed development teams that may include members from different institutions around the world. Cloud-based software development can be quite inexpensive, with many library projects falling within thresholds of free service or at least where monthly subscription fees fall well below direct and indirect costs of local equipment. Cloud computing generally offers a very attractive total cost of ownership value, yet projects involving very large-scale data sets fall into a bracket where cloud computing costs greatly exceed local storage options. Unless the applications under development require unusually intensive levels of resources, it may be possible to stay within the thresholds of use offered without cost.

In this chapter, we've worked through a number of considerations that highlight the advantages and disadvantages of cloud computing. Look for advantages and synergies where the technology lines up well with your library's resources and strategies. It might be a good approach to do more with technology in the absence of abundant resources in computer infrastructure and technical personnel. From a cost perspective, cloud computing gains an advantage for organizations with more of an ability to support recurring fees that may not have spare funds for large-scale equipment procurements. From a security perspective, cloud computing will be delivered through industrial-strength data centers that follow rigorous practices that stand above the capacity of most library IT departments. Libraries involved with highly sensitive information may gravitate toward private rather than public cloud offerings. Cloud computing delivers high standards of reliability, again exceeding what can be accomplished on local equipment. Yet, cloud-based deployments must also plan for failures, with appropriate disaster recovery, backup procedures, and fail-over contingencies. Environmentally, cloud computing is associated with more efficient use of computing resources, reducing a library's energy use and, extrapolated on a wider scale, a broad decrease in energy consumption. Another benefit lies in the flexibility for library developers to quickly gain access to the resources they need or to work easily in decentralized teams. The downside of cloud computing lies in less local control of computing resources and increased reliance on the Internet for access to critical systems. Libraries should be aware of all of these trade-offs as they consider incorporating cloud computing into their technology strategies.

6
Planning for Cloud Computing

Technology should be a component of the operational and budgetary planning that a library executes in support of its strategic mission. Careful thought should be given to its computing and network infrastructure, the business applications that support its operations, and the technologies involved in the delivery of services to its end users. Cloud computing adds an additional option to the palette of available technologies for the library as it formulates its strategic environment. No technology should be implemented solely because it is new and trendy, but because it is based on a solid business case. A technology such as cloud computing should be adopted when it can be demonstrated that it offers the best functionality and value with the least risk. In this chapter we will look at issues that libraries should consider in their planning process that come into play with cloud computing.

Libraries need to plan for the changes associated with this major shift in technology away from components installed locally toward those delivered through some type of cloud-based service. The degree of impact will

An earlier version of this chapter was published in *Cloud Computing for Libraries* (The Tech Set #11).

vary according to how quickly the library navigates this shift and whether the applications involved provide critical operational support or relate to more incidental types of activities. Switching to an ILS delivered through SaaS requires much more planning than deciding to make use of free cloud services such as Dropbox or Google Apps.

AN INEVITABLE FUTURE?

It should be emphasized that the movement toward delivery of technology through cloud computing is, at least to a certain extent, inevitable. Two decades ago, we saw mainframe computers fall out of favor and eventually become obsolete. The time came when the costs associated with maintaining this model of computing could no longer be sustained as less expensive and more efficient alternatives emerged. In the same way, cloud computing seems to be positioned to grow into an increasing level of dominance. In the realm of library systems, many of the newer products are offered only through SaaS.

Even if the library does not have short-term projects under consideration to implement new systems where cloud computing might be an option, long-term planning should take this technology trend into consideration. Over the next decade, most libraries can expect their technology budgets to drift toward subscription-based services and away from local infrastructure.

REBALANCE BUDGETS FOR TECHNOLOGY

The transition to cloud computing has major implications in the way that libraries plan and execute their budgets and allocate resources. Most libraries fund technology projects through a combination of regular budget allocations and up-front costs paid through capital budgets. Local computing infrastructure generally requires significant up-front investments. Initial costs would include the purchase of hardware components such as high-performance servers, redundant disk storage, uninterruptible power sources, tape drives and media for data backup, as well as licenses for the application and supporting components such as operating systems, database management systems, reporting engines, and security products. In addition to these up-front costs, ongoing service and support fees would be part of the annual operating budget. As a broad rule of thumb, the annual maintenance payments are generally around 15 percent of the initial license fee. Every five years or so, the library will need to plan additional capital costs for server replacement and operating system upgrades.

The implementation of similar applications through SaaS assumes a different, much simpler budget model. Instead of the combination of up-front capital expenditures, periodic hardware replacement costs, and annual maintenance fees, the library will need to plan for a single, all-inclusive annual subscription fee. Libraries can expect that the subscription fee associated with SaaS will be higher than the maintenance fee paid for locally hosted applications. This subscription fee covers access to the software, hosting, and support.

As some or all of its computing infrastructure moves to cloud models, the library's budget planning will need to take into consideration the need for higher subscription fees paid annually, which will be offset by savings in periodic purchases of hardware. Less local hardware may also translate into savings in personnel, as noted earlier.

CONSIDER COSTS

Local computing requires the purchase of computing equipment that brings with it a set of expenses, including the purchase of the equipment itself, personnel to maintain it, facilities to house and cool it, service plan fees, and eventually replacement costs. As a general approach, cloud computing trades all of those cost components for monthly subscription fees, either fixed or variable according to consumption. Whether the cost model associated with cloud computing counts as an advantage or disadvantage for the library depends on two factors, local budget preferences and value. From a budget management perspective, the issue hinges on whether funding models favor constant payouts at a moderate level versus higher start-up costs with lower ongoing direct expenses. Stated another way, would a monthly subscription fee for SaaS be easier to accommodate than the start-up costs associated with purchasing a server and software licenses but paying a lower monthly amount for maintenance annually? Some libraries find it easier to obtain one-time funding for projects but have low operating budgets. Grant funding might be available to cover the purchase of equipment but not for longer-term operational costs. For others, the opportunities for one-time project funding may be limited while operational budgets can accommodate reasonable operational expenses.

It's also essential to understand whether local computing or cloud-based alternatives offer the best value in terms of a long-term total cost of ownership analysis. Calculated over a period representing the full life span of the project, how will all the direct and indirect costs associated with local infrastructure compare with the total subscription fees paid for cloud-based services? If one approach offers a higher total cost of ownership than the other, then the library must then carefully decide whether any functional advantages might outweigh the financial issues. Increased local control, for example, might be a result that a library might be willing to pay extra to achieve if the financial analysis came out in favor of SaaS. Strategic repositioning of library technology staff could justify somewhat higher costs of moving to cloud-based deployment of routine infrastructure components. So, while libraries may not always choose the cheapest alternative, they must seek the best value.

NEGOTIATE SERVICE-LEVEL AGREEMENTS

Any time that an organization subscribes to a set of cloud-based services as part of its critical infrastructure, it should pay careful attention to the terms of the subscription contract that specify exactly what guarantees come with the services provided. A contract for computing resources through a cloud provider will naturally specify what resources will be provided to the customer and what fees the customer will pay. These contracts should also include service-level agreements that specify the allowable percentages of downtime, response times for service issues, the performance of transactions, and other metrics that quantify acceptable delivery of the computing resources and what remedies the provider will implement should the service levels fall below the stated requirements.

It's also important to keep in mind that major problems can take place without triggering service-level agreements. When an organization contracts for raw computing resources through IaaS, it continues to be responsible for the proper functioning of its software applications and data integrity. If a library operates its ILS in a cloud infrastructure such as Amazon's EC2 service, and it experiences a software malfunction that results in corrupt data and downtime of its catalog, it's unlikely that Amazon would bear any actionable responsibility. Operating applications in a cloud environment does not mitigate the need to implement adequate contingency planning for data backup and restoration procedures.

In addition to negotiating the best service-level agreement, the library will need to plan any necessary contingencies beyond its terms. Even if the agreement specifies that the provider will perform and maintain backup copies of data, the library may want to also implement replicates of the data outside the service provider. The library may choose to regularly copy data to media it holds locally or to another storage service provider. These measures can mitigate risk in the event of a technical error, business failure, or other events that might cause a disruption in the service.

RECOGNIZE CLOUD COMPUTING'S IMPLICATIONS FOR INTERNET BANDWIDTH

Cloud computing makes a major impact on an organization's use of Internet bandwidth. It will increase the organization's dependence on its Internet connectivity and will result in increases in the bandwidth used. The pathways of access differ fundamentally when deployed through a cloud-based service compared to local infrastructure. The traffic between end users and the service flows through the provider's Internet connections instead of the library's more limited connection. Likewise, library personnel will connect to the service via the Internet rather than through the library's local network. Assuming that the traffic involved to support end users exceeds that for in-library use, the provision of services through cloud-based services should decrease the organization's overall bandwidth consumption. Especially for high-volume web-based services, a remotely hosted deployment may save the organization considerable expense in its telecommunication costs associated with upgrading Internet bandwidth. A service based on cloud infrastructure in most cases should also result in much higher performance and reliability than would be possible through an organization's local Internet connection. Providers of cloud-based services maintain very high bandwidth connections to the Internet, typically through multiple providers. Most large-scale data centers associated with cloud service providers have sufficient redundant connectivity that even if their primary Internet connection suffers a disruption, access continues through alternate pathways.

These differences in the patterns of Internet bandwidth should be considered when planning for technology infrastructure and corresponding budgets. A library needs to constantly monitor its incoming and outgoing bandwidth and at least on an annual basis make adjustments with its Internet service provider to ensure that it has adequate capacity to meet demand.

Even when its core services are provided externally through cloud-based services, the library's connectivity to the Internet continues to serve a critical role. This connection connects all in-library computers to the Internet, including workstations provided for library patrons and computers used by library personnel, as well as wireless networks provided for public access. A library's Internet connection needs to be sized not only to support connectivity to any applications that it may have deployed through external service providers, but it also must provide access to an increasing number of remote electronic resources. As more of these resources come in the form of multimedia audio and video, bandwidth demands may increase considerably.

SHIFT TO LIBRARY AUTOMATION IN THE CLOUD

Libraries make major investments in the core automation systems that help them manage their operations and provide access to their collections and services. The ILS, also called the library management system in regions outside the United States, delivers automation support for the operations of the library, especially in the areas of acquiring, cataloging, and circulating collection materials, and offers access and self-service features to library users through its built-in online catalog. Discovery products provide access to a wider view of library collections, going beyond the materials managed directly within the ILS to include other digital collections and the resources available through the library's subscriptions to electronic content products. Given the strategic importance and the financial investments that libraries make in their core automation and discovery platforms, it's essential that they operate in the most efficient ways and make use of the most appropriate technologies. It's essential to explore and take advantage of the most efficient and appropriate technology models. These issues of choosing the best technology architectures and deployment models apply to each of the major components in a library's strategic technology environment, including ILSs, discovery interfaces, institutional repositories, asset management systems, and digital preservation platforms.

A shift from locally implemented automation systems to alternatives that deliver equivalent functionality through cloud-based services can make a dramatic impact on the way that a library manages its technology resources. Reliance on SaaS instead of operating local equipment reorients personnel away from dealing with servers, operating systems, and other infrastructure issues toward more concentration on higher-level functional and strategic activities.

While the implementation of cloud computing makes a major difference to organizations or departments involved in providing and supporting technology, it will largely be transparent to the organizations and individuals that make use of the resulting products. The shift to cloud computing might completely redefine the part of a library organization responsible for the management of its automation systems. The administrative unit of a consortium or of a public or university library system, for example, might operate an ILS and other applications on behalf of a set of branches and facilities that comprise the organization. Moving to SaaS is tantamount to outsourcing significant portions of the support structures.

Libraries that share computing resources managed by a consortium, branches of a public library system, divisional libraries, or others that use but don't manage an automation system should experience little change. The way that these libraries make use of the system will change very little depending on whether the system is managed by their central administrative unit or through a vendor-hosted SaaS arrangement.

CONSIDER APPLICATION SERVICE PROVIDER OFFERINGS

The customer library accesses the system through the Internet, using the same client software as would be used with a local installation, which might be a graphical user interface running under Windows, Mac, or Linux, a Java-based graphical client, or a purely web-based interface. In this flavor of SaaS, the provider will operate a separate instance of the software for each library system or consortium, which distinguishes it from multi-tenant SaaS where many unrelated organizations participate in a shared instance. This allows a library to gain benefits such as relief from local hosting, hardware and operating support, and subscription pricing while using well-established automation products.

Libraries involved with a traditional ILS that they have implemented locally will eventually find the need to upgrade or replace the server hardware. Many libraries may find the approaching demise of older server hardware as an opportunity to reassess whether they should relinquish their self-hosting arrangement and shift to an application service provider arrangement. Almost all of the major ILS vendors offer hosted versions of their products and often will give significant incentives to adopt this approach rather than local installations. The delivery of ILSs through application service provider arrangements, in recent years positioned as a version of SaaS, has been a routine alternative for over a decade, with an ever-increasing number of libraries choosing this approach.

SirsiDynix, one of the largest library automation vendors globally, emphasizes SaaS as one of its strategic deployment options. The company markets its major automation and discovery products through SaaS, including the Symphony and Horizon library management systems, the Enterprise discovery platform, and the Portfolio digital asset management system. SirsiDynix has focused its recent development efforts on its BLUEcloud suite, a set of web-based modules deployed through a multi-tenant platform that operate in tandem with existing Symphony or Horizon ILS implementations. While BLUEcloud is not an all-inclusive ILS, it offers selected modules through web-based interfaces as well as providing new functionality. The eResource Central BLUEcloud module provides a web-based utility for the management and access of e-books and other electronic resources. A vast majority of SirsiDynix customers are choosing an SaaS option, both those moving from local installations of the same product as well as those implementing the system for the first time. The initial versions of the Enterprise discovery interface were available only through SaaS; only in more recent versions can libraries install the software locally. Portfolio's orientation toward SaaS as the primary development and deployment model reflects this company's strategy as the prevailing industry trend.

The transition from locally managed systems to vendor hosting has been a long-term trend in the industry. At least three of the predecessor companies that now constitute SirsiDynix became involved in application service provider offerings beginning in about 2000, when Sirsi Corporation began offering its Unicorn ILS through Sirsi.net, which was also the year that epixtech,

Inc. (later Dynix Corporation) became an application service provider for the Horizon ILS; Data Research Associates began its application service provider product in 2000. Ex Libris has offered Aleph, MetaLib, and SFX in application service provider configurations since 2000; this company launched Voyager-Plus in early 2011, a fully hosted and managed service based on the Voyager ILS, and offers Primo Total Care, a hosted version of its core discovery platform. VTLS has offered its Virtua ILS through an application service provider since 2003.

Innovative Interfaces may have been the first to offer an application service provider deployment of an ILS when it launched its INN-Keeper service in April 1997 with the Western State University College of Law and the Thomas Jefferson School of Law as early adopters.

Civica Library and Learning is an international company that offers the Spydus library management system in both locally installed and hosted versions. Outside the United States, the application service provider model is usually called "managed services." Over half of the libraries using the Spydus library management system have implemented the managed service option.

Similar hosting arrangements are also available for open source library automation systems. Most libraries that implement an open source library automation system, such as Koha or Evergreen, rely on conversion, installation, and support services from a commercial provider. A large portion of these installations also rely on the support firm to provide hosting services, resulting in an implementation quite similar to the application service provider offerings seen with the proprietary systems. Koha and Evergreen both incorporate designs that lend themselves to individual instances of the application established for each library system or consortium that adopts the system rather than shared instances.

Some of the vendor-hosted installations of open source automation systems make use of IaaS. LibLime, for example, deploys its LibLime Academic Koha using Amazon EC2, providing a high-performance environment for its clients. LibLime reports that it deploys over 90 percent of its installations through this model of SaaS.

CONSIDER MULTI-TENANT SOFTWARE-AS-A-SERVICE

Library automation applications designed and developed in more recent years incorporate more current technology architectures, including adherence to the service-oriented architecture, more reliance on web-based interfaces instead of graphical clients, and orientation toward multi-tenant SaaS. Library automation applications designed under the client/server architecture targeting one installation per library, library system, or consortium implementing the system cannot easily be transformed into more pure deployments of SaaS where a single instance is designed to serve multiple independent organizations making use of the software. These traditional applications can gain many of the benefits of SaaS through vendor-hosted application service provider arrangements, but they fall short of delivering the full menu of benefits the more modern approach affords. In this section we will review some of the library automation products that embrace the more modern understanding of SaaS that goes beyond vendor hosting of traditional software.

Ex Libris (www.exlibrisgroup.com), though most of its previous generation products were designed for traditional deployment, has fully embraced cloud technologies for its current offerings. Its Aleph and Voyager ILSs target academic and research libraries, most of which install the software on local computing infrastructure. Ex Libris has offered Voyager only since early 2011 through a fully managed hosted service. The company's discovery product Primo, launched in 2006, was designed for individual local installations, though since 2010 it has offered a hosted version branded as Primo TotalCare. In 2009 Ex Libris created a consolidated index of article-level content, named Primo Central, to expand the capabilities of the core Primo discovery interface. Primo Central, though not a separate software product, is deployed using cloud-based technologies in an instance of Primo shared by all libraries that subscribe to the service

Alma (www.exlibrisgroup.com/category/AlmaOverview), Ex Libris's current resource management platform, fully embraces cloud computing. Released initially in early 2012, Alma is deployed as a multi-tenant SaaS using all web-based clients and deployed via IaaS. The data model of Alma includes broadly shared resources, called the Community Zone, accessible by all libraries that participate in the service. It also includes the ability to support partitions of data specific to each library, called the Local Zone, for inventory and collections specific to the organization implementing the product. A Network Zone provides common data shared among libraries implementing Alma in common as shared resource management infrastructure. Increasingly library consortia have chosen Alma as shared infrastructure, including the Orbis Cascade Alliance, the California State University System, the WHELF consortium of academic libraries in Wales, and many others.

Biblionix (www.biblionix.com), a Texas-based company, provides a library automation product called Apollo to small public libraries through SaaS. Biblionix explains that Apollo was designed as a true multi-tenant SaaS application, with each instance capable of supporting all the libraries that use the product. It operates multiple instances, however, for the purpose of load balancing and to provide redundancy to increase the reliability of the services. Biblionix reports that it benefits from having all its customers run the same version of the service, with new versions and features deployed simultaneously. Another added advantage involves the ability to simplify interactions with external vendors, such as for connections to interlibrary loan systems. Apollo provides an example of how SaaS can be leveraged to produce a web-based library automation system for small public libraries at an affordable cost.

The Kuali OLE project (http://kuali.org/ole) is an open source, enterprise-oriented library automation environment for academic and research libraries, with partial funding through a grant from the Andrew W. Mellon Foundation. Though the finished product will be initially deployed on local infrastructure at each of the organizations in the partnership, the project makes extensive use of cloud technologies, exemplifying the advantages of this technology for software development. The Kuali OLE project engaged HTC Global Services, a software development firm with offshore programmers in India, to perform software design, coding, and quality assurance tasks. The use of Amazon's cloud-based infrastructure provides support for this globally distributed software development endeavor. Programming takes place in India using Agile methodologies that produce code quickly for small components of the system in rapid succession. The development partner libraries test each iteration of new functionality from locations throughout the United States. The project has been a proving ground for the ability of cloud technologies to provide a flexible development environment. Project participants indicate that the use of this shared cloud-based infrastructure has been much more efficient than would be the case if the changes had to be installed on servers for each institution involved with the project.

In recent years, additional components complement the ILS, such as discovery products and services. With a broader scope than the content managed within the ILS and with more modern features, discovery systems have supplanted the online catalog modules for an increasing number of libraries. While some discovery services may function as next-generation library catalogs, offering a more modern interface to basically the same content as the integrated library system, many—especially those oriented to academic libraries—offer comprehensive indexes that span the library's traditional print collection, plus individual articles represented in subscriptions to electronic content products, institutional repositories, and collections of digital materials. As with the ILS, the deployment options of discovery products include local installations, with a growing trend toward SaaS offerings.

BiblioCommons (www.bibliocommons.com), a discovery interface for public libraries based on social networking concepts, is delivered through a multi-tenant SaaS platform. BiblioCommons was developed by a company of the same name based in Toronto, Ontario, Canada. The product was initially implemented primarily by libraries in Canada, such as the Oakville Public Library, which served as the pilot site beginning in July 2009, and by the Edmonton Public Library and others in the provinces of Alberta, British Columbia, and Ontario. BiblioCommons has also been implemented in libraries throughout the United States, and in New Zealand. Other major municipal libraries in North America implementing BiblioCommons include Charlotte

ACCESS TO APIs

In addition to the web-based or graphical interfaces provided with an ILS, many libraries take advantage of APIs to support connections to other business systems or to accommodate local programming to accomplish ad hoc reporting or other extensions of functionality.

When considering an ILS through an SaaS deployment, libraries that expect access to APIs need to determine the extent to which they are available. There may be differences between the levels of access to APIs offered on vendor-hosted systems relative to what is possible with local installations. Libraries that intend to use a third-party discovery interface, for example, will need to be sure that all the data synchronization capabilities and APIs required will be available.

Mecklenburg Library, Chicago Public, Brooklyn Public, Seattle Public, Boston Public, San Francisco Public Library, King County Library System, Multnomah County Library, and many other large urban and suburban library systems. It has been implemented by the Christchurch City Libraries in New Zealand and the Yarra Plenty Regional Library in Australia. A single instance of the BiblioCommons platform serves all the libraries subscribing to the service. BiblioCommons includes a suite of application programming interfaces (APIs) that allow libraries to develop their own applications against the platform and to connect with external systems. Each library that subscribes to BiblioCommons makes use of customized indexes derived from their local collections, with connections into the ILS that dynamically present the status and location of any item viewed and to present patron services such as hold requests and renewals.

BiblioCommons embraces all the characteristics of a true SaaS, including multiple organizations sharing a single instance, but with the ability to implement local branding, configuration, customizations, and delivery of the application through a web-based interface.

REPOSITORIES MOVE TO THE CLOUD TECHNOLOGIES

Libraries can also implement institutional repository functions, digital collections, and digital preservation activities through cloud technologies. Two of the primary open source platforms for institutional repositories, DSpace and the Fedora Commons, merged into a common governance organization called DuraSpace (www.duraspace.org). In addition to ongoing development and maintenance, the DuraSpace organization created a new product based on both technologies called DuraCloud (http://duracloud.org). As implied by its name, it will employ cloud technologies to deliver a flexible service for storage, long-term digital preservation, and access to objects in a digital repository. The levels of protection required to support rigorous standards of preservation are accomplished by storing each object through multiple cloud storage service providers, including Amazon S3, Rackspace CloudFiles, and EMC Atmos. The DuraCloud service includes a DuraStore web application that provides an interface into the storage services that manage the digital objects, including the distribution and validation of copies across the multiple cloud storage services. Another set of services supports access to the digital objects through the creation of derivative images, streaming video, and other tasks related to accessing and viewing the objects. DuraSpace and LYRASIS intend to merge. Together, their hosted services would include ArchivesSpace, CollectionSpace, Islandora, DuraCloud, DSpaceDirect, and ArchivesDirect.

OCLC EMBRACES THE CLOUD

Of all the organizations providing technology and data services to libraries, OCLC has some of the strongest associations with cloud computing. OCLC's mantra asserts that libraries will increase their impact as they move from isolated individual systems to a globally shared infrastructure and that it stands in a unique position to deliver this capacity to libraries, building on the organization's mission, worldwide presence, and massive data resources. The organization's core bibliographic database, WorldCat, stands as the world's largest repository of library metadata and is the basis of cataloging services for OCLC's member libraries throughout the world. OCLC has steadily expanded the services surrounding WorldCat to include resource sharing and interlibrary loan. WorldCat Local was launched as a discovery service in 2007. In 2009, OCLC announced its ambitious agenda to take WorldCat to yet another level of functionality to include circulation, acquisitions, license management, and other features that would allow it to function as a library's comprehensive automation environment. Its current product, now known as WorldShare Management Services, eliminates the need for a library to operate a local ILS. OCLC based its development strategy of WorldShare Management Services on a new technology infrastructure that theoretically would be capable of handling the transactions of all the libraries in the world and would leverage the WorldCat database of bibliographic records to support item-level transactions. Libraries opting to implement OCLC's WorldShare Management Services use web-based clients to perform tasks otherwise associated with ILS modules such as circulation, cataloging, and acquisitions. The data models involved contrast with traditional automation products in that all libraries share bibliographic records in WorldCat, attaching holdings and items as needed. The concept of importing or transferring bibliographic records into a local system no longer applies, because no local system needs to exist with this approach.

WorldShare Management Services fits into several aspects of the cloud-based computing models. Deployed as multi-tenant SaaS, it eliminates the need for a library to operate its own local automation system. It is operated entirely through web-based clients, including both staff and end-user access. All organizations that make use of the service participate in a single shared instance. The data related to the operation of WorldShare Management Services resides entirely within OCLC's infrastructure.

OCLC operates WorldShare Management Services on computing infrastructure it owns and maintains rather than on IaaS provided through a third party. OCLC has a long history of maintaining large-scale computing services and has created redundant, geographically distributed fail-over facilities should problems arise with its primary data center housed at its headquarters in Dublin, Ohio.

One of the key characteristics of WorldShare Management Services relates to the data services provided. In addition to the well-known World-Cat bibliographic database, the product will make use of many other shared repositories of data, providing much greater efficiencies than alternatives in which each library maintains its own local files. Examples include a shared repository of vendors from which libraries acquire materials. Through the use of a shared vendor registry, libraries can tag onto an existing vendor record for their orders, adding any library-specific elements when needed. The general data structure of WorldShare Management Services allows libraries to make use of globally shared records, with the ability to add local information and with granular controls in place to restrict the libraries using the system from viewing or altering another library's local information. Other examples of shared data structures within WorldShare Management Services include the WorldCat knowledge base that includes data on e-content products in support of electronic resource management and in the discovery and linking needed for end-user services. WorldShare Management Services provides support for the internal operations of a library. While WorldCat Local most easily integrates with it as the library's discovery interface, other third-party products could be used as well.

In addition to the basic functionality that OCLC delivers through World-Share Management Services, it also anticipates that libraries will want to create additional tools and services to fulfill local needs. OCLC offers a set of APIs that allow libraries to tap into data and functionality resources through the WorldShare Platform. Through this set of APIs, OCLC delivers a platform to support third-party applications that might be created by libraries, vendors, or other organizations. OCLC facilitates a developer's network by providing a collaborative environment to foster development activities.

WorldShare Management Services presses cloud-based library automation to its logical conclusion. The product entered the early adoption cycle in 2010.

DETERMINE THE COST OF LIBRARY AUTOMATION IN THE CLOUD

One of the fundamental realities of budget planning for large technology projects involves the absence of published price lists for software and related services. Vendors scale prices according to the size and complexity of the organization and to the specific modules and options selected. Although some rough formula may be used to calculate a base price, the final offer may also include factors relative to specific competitive bidding scenarios. Prices may also change in the process of contract negotiations. Some of the factors that come into play in the pricing for major business applications such as an ILS include the following.

The population served by the organization implementing the application. For academic libraries the relevant metric might include the full-time enrollment of the college or university; for public libraries the number of registered patrons would apply.

The number of personnel operating the software, which may be expressed as the number of copies licensed for the staff client software. Variables to consider include whether this is the total number of potential users of the software or the maximum number of simultaneous users.

The size of the collections managed, including the number of metadata records and total items or objects.

The modules or options selected. For an ILS, the library will select which of the major modules it requires, such as cataloging, circulation, serials management, acquisitions, or online catalog. Other components that may involve additional cost include system-to-system interfaces such as enabling the SIP2 (system interchange protocol, version 2) protocol for self-service stations, NCIP (NISO Circulation Interchange Protocol) for interlibrary loan or resource sharing, Z39.50 client to search and download bibliographic records from external sources, and Z39.50 server to enable search of the system by external applications. Access to the full set of APIs may involve an additional fee to enable access as well as costs for mandatory training programs.

BUDGET MODEL FOR SOFTWARE-AS-A-SERVICE

A pure SaaS environment can offer a budget model as simple as a set monthly or annual subscription fee. While this subscription fee may be higher than what a library might be accustomed to pay for the maintenance of locally installed applications, it's important to keep in mind the offsetting costs.

Even in an SaaS arrangement, there may be some other costs that need to be included in budget planning. In the migration from an existing ILS to a new one delivered through SaaS, there may be transition costs. Depending on the circumstances, exit fees may apply to the incumbent system for data extraction or other services that may be needed as the organization terminates its use.

Application software vendors may reasonably expect that organizations that use the APIs go through certification or training courses, because their improper use can result in data corruption problems that their customer support departments would need to rectify.

As seen in this chapter, cloud-based options permeate the products and services related to library automation and resource discovery. Established products that predate current expectations for SaaS can be deployed through vendor-hosted arrangements that deliver similar benefits. The movement toward cloud computing goes beyond the core management system; applications across all the different areas that support library operations, collection management, and patron interfaces are increasingly offered through options other than the traditional approach of installation on local servers. This chapter included numerous examples, across several product categories, but should not be considered an exhaustive survey.

The trend toward cloud-based library automation also should not be taken in a way that devalues the incumbent model that relies on software installed on local servers. For many libraries, the local computing model will continue to work quite well for many years to come. Those that require a high degree of local control, have sufficient personnel for managing technical infrastructure, that require highly customized applications, or that have jurisdictional or policy requirements that restrict the way they store institutional data may not be in a position to take advantage of key automation systems deployed through cloud technologies. Over the next decade, however, if current trends prevail, the number of products offered primarily through SaaS will increase as will the proportions of libraries opting for this approach.

7
Introduction to Library
Service Platforms

This chapter aims to provide a general understanding of library service platforms and to provide libraries with additional data and perspective as they consider the options available in developing their technology strategies. Library services platforms have not replaced previously established categories wholesale and for all types of libraries. Integrated library systems continue to flourish as seen by ongoing use of existing installations and in new sales. Each type and size of library comes with its own concerns and requirements that it expects to be addressed by its technology products. While library services platforms may be appropriate for a growing set of libraries, any data that demonstrates the types of libraries using any given product can be helpful as libraries ponder their options.

Libraries making decisions about products should consult with a variety of sources as they work through their procurement process. The report provides general descriptions and presents empirical data related to the numbers and types of libraries that have implemented each product. Sources of

An earlier version of this chapter was published in *Library Technology Reports* (May/June 2015).

data include previously published statistics, figures provided by the vendors of the products, the libraries.org library directory, and the annual "Library Automation Perceptions Survey," available at librarytechnology.org. While general descriptions of the products are given, the report does not attempt to list or characterize the detailed functionality of the products covered. An understanding of the specific features of each product and its suitability to any given library can be gained only through more in-depth product research. Consider this a snapshot meant to illustrate a class of product.

In describing the characteristics of a library services platform, I'll reference OCLC WorldShare Management Services, Ex Libris Alma, Sierra from Innovative Interfaces, Kuali OLE, and SirsiDynix BLUEcloud Suite.

WHAT IS A LIBRARY SERVICES PLATFORM?

The term *library services platform* describes a type of library resource management system with a set of characteristics that differ substantially from the long-standing genre of integrated library systems. At this time, there was considerable concern about integrated library systems not necessarily meeting expectations, and it was helpful to consider the new generation of products as a new category that did not have the conceptual and functional baggage of the existing set of products. But the introduction of the term has also introduced some confusion, especially since many products fit some of its characteristics and not others. Above all, as we consider library services platforms, it must be noted that it describes a set of products that each embody a somewhat different set of conceptual, technical, and functional characteristics. While I continue to see library services platform as a helpful term to describe this set of products, the lines of distinction remain blurry.

We refer to any major product that a library uses to manage some set of its collection as a resource management system. This broad category includes library services platforms, integrated library systems, electronic resource management systems, and digital collections management systems, as well as those products that may be used for other categories of specialized materials.

I coined the term *library services platform* in 2011 to describe a new set of products that was being developed that promised to take a much different approach to library resource management than the incumbent integrated library systems.

I initially proposed the term in my August 2011 "Smarter Libraries through Technology" column in *Smart Libraries Newsletter*:

> I'm gravitating toward the term "library services platform" for this new software genre. The products are library-specific, they enable the library to perform its services, internally and externally though their

built-in functionality, as well as exposing a platform of Web services and other APIs for interoperability and custom development. In a time when long-standing terms like "integrated library system" or OPAC bring along considerable negative baggage, we need new terms when we talk about what comes next.[1]

My September 2011 "Systems Librarian" column in *Computers in Libraries* further refined the concept:

> This new generation of products—more appropriately called something like library services platforms rather than integrated library systems— addresses the fundamental changes that libraries have experienced over the course of the last decade or so toward more engagement with electronic and digital content. In their own distinctive ways, these recently announced or delivered systems aim to break free of the models of automation centered mostly on print materials deeply embodied by the incumbent line of integrated library systems. To make up for functionality absent in their core integrated library systems, many libraries implemented a cluster of ancillary products, such as link resolvers, electronic resource management systems, digital asset management systems, and other repository platforms to manage all their different types of materials. The new products aim to simplify library operations through a more inclusive platform designed to handle all the different forms of content.[2]

The introduction of the term *library services platform* was also meant to provide a vendor-neutral product category. As each of these products was being introduced, each vendor posited its own name for its approach. Ex Libris used Unified Resource Management, and OCLC used Web-Scale Management Service. Vendors tend not to use each other's product categories for new products, so providing a neutral term was needed. The term has since been adopted in both the library and vendor communities.

HISTORIC PERSPECTIVE: CONSOLIDATION OF FUNCTIONALITY

The general missions of libraries have remained fairly constant throughout the history of these institutions. They develop collections of materials of interest to their communities and provide ways to make those materials available. The types and formats of materials that comprise their collections and how they have been stored, organized, and made available have changed with each era of publishing and content distribution. In each phase of the history of libraries, they have made use of the tools and technologies of the time to facilitate their work.

The history of library technology tracks alongside the prevailing technologies available in the general business and consumer sectors. Methods employed by libraries have constantly evolved. Though we don't aim to delve too deeply into the history of library automation, some of the tools employed prior to the age of computing include handwritten sequential catalogs, printed catalog volumes, and card catalogs. Computers allowed libraries to manage and provide access to their collections more easily. Early products included computer output microfilm. The early mainframe computers were also put to use to help libraries automate the circulation, cataloging, and acquisitions of their collections. Programs dedicated to individual areas of library operations eventually coalesced into integrated library systems that addressed multiple areas of functionality based on centralized databases. Library-oriented applications have been developed and redeveloped through each of the generations of technology, from mainframes to client/server applications and more recently into those based on cloud computing and web-based technologies. The functionality addressed has likewise morphed over this period, with new products emerging to support the library involvement with electronic and digital materials and in providing ever more effective tools for their management and access.

One theme that has remained constant through the development of library automation systems can be seen in the gradual consolidation of programs and tools that each addresses a given area of the library's work into more integrated or unified platforms. Each phase of libraries brings new operational tasks that benefit from technology, leading to new products to meet those needs. In subsequent phases, new products emerge that subsume much of the functionality of these multiple applications, resulting in more streamlined and integrated platforms.

The realm of computing technology culminated in the late 1970s with the development of integrated library systems. The individual programs dedicated to individual areas of library operations eventually coalesced into business applications that addressed multiple areas of functionality based on centralized databases. Separate applications for each area of the library were consolidated into the first generation of integrated library systems. The earliest phase of library automation was characterized by specialized systems for each main area of library processing. Gaylord offered its Circulation 100 and CLSI offered LIBS100, which primarily addressed the circulation of books. Innovative Interfaces, Inc., offered its INNOVAQ product, which specialized in materials acquisitions. Libraries at this time could have products from different vendors to automate their operations. Each of these products, and new entrants into the arena, developed into full-fledged integrated library systems.

The ongoing evolution of publishing and content creation continually makes an impact on the types of materials collected by libraries. Libraries have increasingly become more involved with print and digital materials, thus creating the need for new tools and technologies to acquire, manage, and provide access to them.

The first decade of the twenty-first century saw a new phase of fragmentation in library technologies. The integrated library system was well established as the core automation system, adopted in all but the smallest of public and academic libraries in the developed world. As libraries began to acquire electronic resources, new tools were needed for each aspect of the management of and access to those materials.

Integrated library systems, although comprehensive for the acquisition, management, and access to primarily print materials, saw their role in the overall technology environment of a library diminished for those libraries that shifted their collections acquisitions to primarily electronic and digital resources. See the section "Library Services Platform or Integrated Library System" later in this chapter for more details.

OpenURL link resolvers emerged in the early 2000s to assist libraries in providing a manageable approach to linking from citations to the full text or other services to make articles available to library users. These products were able to provide context-sensitive linking to the full text on the server of the publisher to which the library subscribes. Hard-coded links used prior to the emergence of link resolvers were unsustainable due to the massive numbers of e-journals and articles to which libraries provide access and in the enormous effort required each time the library changed its subscriptions or when a publisher adjusted its servers.

Knowledge bases of electronic resources provide a database that describes the content packages to which libraries subscribe. The knowledge base provides current lists of each of the e-journals included in any aggregated content product and the years covered, the syntax needed to link to individual articles, and many other details related to the body of library-oriented electronic content. These knowledge bases support OpenURL link resolvers and other applications that benefit from data related to e-resource holdings. A knowledge base of e-journal holdings describes the totality of the content potentially available to libraries. Link resolvers would include a profile of the library's subscriptions to inform its ability to provide direct links to items available to a library patron directly or to offer alternative services for those not found within the library's collection of subscriptions.[3]

A–Z listings and other finding aids are often associated with link resolvers and make use of the e-resource knowledge base.

Electronic resource management systems provide specialized capabilities for acquisition, description, and other operational tasks associated with aggregated content products, e-journals, and other packages of electronic content. These products usually rely on a knowledge base of e-content products to simplify management activities. Electronic resource management systems provide functionality not traditionally included in an integrated library system, such as coding and tracking of license terms, collection of usage statistics, analysis of the value and performance of content packages, and other functionality specific to this type of content. Electronic resource management systems include financial management components to manage expenditures relative to established library budgets. They have to handle multiple procurement models, including standard annual subscriptions, open-access selections, purchase of backfile collections, and other scenarios.

Libraries may also maintain one or more publishing or repository platforms where they store, describe, and manage documents or other content objects on behalf of their institutions. These publishing platforms might include repositories for electronic theses and dissertations or institutional repositories for holding local copies of published scholarly articles, research reports, institutional publications, and other materials. Digital asset management systems or other platforms for managing collections are needed for libraries with digitization initiatives for manuscripts, photographs, or other materials or for managing natively digital content.

Digital preservation platforms provide additional layers of functionality to a digital asset management environment to ensure the long-term viability of digital materials.

The emergence of library services platforms brings another round of consolidation of functionality that brings together several categories of functionality that had been handled in separate products. The library services platform in general will replace multiple incumbent products, including the integrated library system, any formal or informal products or processes to manage electronic resources, and knowledge bases of e-content resources. These platforms can also address link resolution, though this functionality spans a gray area between resource management and discovery.

Library services platforms should not be considered monolithic self-contained systems that become the only technology product a library will need. We have noted that library services platforms generally do not handle discovery, though many providers will offer a library services platform and a discovery service as an integrated suite. The current products also do not necessarily serve as publishing platforms to replace institutional repository or large-scale digital asset management systems. Some of the products may have basic capabilities, but content publishing has not been a main focus of development for these products.

The broader scope of these products must be taken into consideration relative to their cost. It may not be a fair comparison, for example, to evaluate the cost of a library services platform relative to an integrated library system that addresses a narrower scope of resources. The library services platform may replace three or more incumbent systems, usually the integrated library system, the electronic resource management system, and a link resolver and its knowledge base. When delivered as a web-based service, it also displaces local servers and their associated hardware, software, environmental, and personnel costs. A much larger portion of a library's technology support infrastructure will be concentrated in a library services platform rather than dispersed among multiple products and processes that may have characterized the incumbent environment.

DEFINITION AND CHARACTERISTICS

A library services platform enables libraries to acquire and manage their collections, spanning multiple formats of content, including at a minimum physical materials and electronic content. These products support multiple procurement processes, including those related to items purchased for permanent ownership, those made available through paid licenses and subscriptions, and those selected from open-access sources. They offer a metadata management environment offering multiple schemas as appropriate for each of the respective material formats, including at a minimum the MARC family of metadata standards and Dublin Core. A library services platform may include an integrated discovery service or support a separately acquired discovery interface by exposing all needed APIs and other interoperability protocols. Library services platforms are offered through a multi-tenant platform, providing all staff and patron functionality through browser-based interfaces. These products provide knowledge bases that represent the body of content extending beyond the library's specific collection.

FUNCTIONAL CHARACTERISTICS

Refining this general definition with more detail, some of the characteristics of a library services platform include the following.

Management of Electronic and Print Formats of Materials

This genre of products consolidates the management of print and electronic materials into a single platform, taking advantage of common data stores, task workflows, and other points of efficiency. Archival materials, institutional records, and large-scale digital assets may eventually be subsumed within library services platforms, but are usually still managed in separate systems.

Replacement of Multiple Incumbent Products

As noted above, the implementation of a library services platform in most cases will displace existing technical infrastructure components, including the integrated library system and electronic resource management systems. For libraries that have not implemented electronic resource management systems, data and processes managed in local spreadsheets and databases can be more structurally managed through the library services platform.

Extensive Metadata Management

The library services platform supports multiple metadata formats as appropriate for each format, including MARC, Dublin Core, or other XML standards. The need to manage multiple formats of collection materials comes with the need to break outside of the exclusive use of the MARC family of metadata standards. A library services platform will support MARC and non-MARC metadata, either through a normalized internal set of data structures or through a mechanism that natively stores different types of records. New metadata formats based on linked data, especially BIBFRAME, have not yet been operationalized, but they provide an example of new and emerging metadata practices that will need to be adopted by all resource management systems in the relatively near future.

Multiple Procurement Workflows

The library services platform supports procurement workflows for purchased, licensed, and open-access materials. One of the limitations of the integrated library system is related to its orientation to procurement processes for direct ownership. As libraries become increasingly involved in the licensing of electronic materials, many aspects of this type of business arrangement did not fit within the structure of the integrated library system. License terms, tracking of individual titles within aggregated packages, and end-user linking mechanisms were usually accomplished in other ways and often by a different set of library personnel. Despite the considerable overlap in some aspects of the process, these separate processes resulted in a fragmented and less operationally efficient workflow. Library services platforms integrate the acquisition and management of electronic and print resources into a common platform, data stores, and task workflows. An initial phase of this integration may come with placing an electronic resource management module within the same interface as that for print management, but the full integration of the management of these different categories of materials in a completely integrated set of business processes more completely satisfies the vision of the library services platform.

Knowledge Bases

The library services platform includes knowledge bases and bibliographic service from which local collections are drawn or defined. The model of the integrated library system assumes a reliance on external resources for the metadata involved in collection description and management. The emergence of electronic resources led to the use of knowledge bases provided with the service that functioned as a built-in metadata repository. Libraries using these products did not have to create their own databases of e-resource holdings, but could rely on a knowledge base maintained by the supplier. The local collection was defined by a profile that appropriately filtered the comprehensive knowledge base into the specific resources held by the library. The library services platform expands this knowledge base approach to a wider set of resources. At least some of the library services platforms include a built-in knowledge base for both print and electronic resources. Examples include WorldCat as the global bibliographic resource upon which WorldShare Management Services relies; Alma, which includes a Community Catalog of resources available to all libraries as they define their local collections; and ProQuest Intota, which relies on an expanded knowledge base that was originally created in support of the company's link resolver and electronic resource management products.

Built-in Collection Analytics

Although integrated library systems usually include a standard set of reporting tools, library services platforms are often able to provide more advanced capabilities for collection analysis and assessment. Those deployed through multi-tenant platforms may be able to not just provide analysis of the library's local collection independently, but to also use broader data from the platform and its knowledge bases.

Conceptual Organization

The organization of functionality of a library services platform may deviate from the traditional ILS modules (cataloging, online catalog, circulation, acquisitions, serials management, authority control). Fulfillment, for example, may be used to represent the tasks and activities related to the lending of physical materials and the provision of access to electronic resources. Metadata management may be used for describing functions that support MARC-based cataloging, describing digital items in Dublin Core, and managing knowledge base profiles for electronic resources.

Discovery

Library services platforms integrate with a discovery service rather than provide a traditional online catalog. Library services platforms differ in their approach to patron interactions compared to integrated library systems. The online catalog module of the integrated library system provides direct access to the collection and patron-oriented features through internal and proprietary mechanisms. Library services platforms have a more indirect relationship with patron interfaces. Discovery services belong to a separate product genre. For most of the library services platforms, the concept of an online catalog does not apply. Library services platforms expose the APIs that enable a discovery service to provide these services. In some cases, the provider of the library services platform also offers a discovery service.

TECHNICAL CHARACTERISTICS

Library services platforms have been developed to follow the prevailing concepts of current technology. While the specific architectures and technology components found within each of the products in the category of library services platforms may differ, some general technical characteristics can be expected.

Beyond Client/Server Computing

The current generation of integrated library systems was developed during the era when client/server computing prevailed. This model of distributed computing continues to be seen in existing applications, but only rarely in newly created products. Software applications may continue to be layered into client and server tiers internally, but that architecture is not conspicuous in end-user deployments. Almost any new software-based product created in recent years would be designed to be deployed as a web-based service rather than software that has to be installed on either institutional or individual computers. The previous era of client/server computing required the installation of software on a server that provides the basic functionality of the system for that organization, including the business logic and data storage needed to support that organization. Each organization that uses that product would have its own separate installation of the software and independent copies of its own databases. The individual users in the organization that operates the software would also need to have software installed on their own computers. These client applications provide the user interface, manage communications with the server component, and may perform additional tasks such as checking for the validity or integrity of data. This client/server architecture provided advantages over the earlier era of mainframe base computing, but it required significant administrative overhead in the need to install and maintain software components.

Multi-Tenant Platforms

A multi-tenant application serves all of the organizations or individuals using it through a single instance. The service is delivered through a single code base, and all users of the application operate from the same version of the underlying software. Data structures are organized to segregate data that pertains to each institutional or individual user or to allow selected data stores to be shared globally. These multi-tenant systems are generally distributed globally, with data centers in different continents. Users in one region access the system from the nearest data center, with the ability to shift access to another should a failure occur. Most modern services rely on multi-tenant deployment, including business-oriented products such as Salesforce.com, e-commerce environments like Amazon.com, social networks such as Facebook, or messaging utilities like Gmail. Multi-tenant applications can support massively large-scale services.

This style of computing is not new to the library arena. Many well-established library-oriented products are offered through multi-tenant platforms:

- WorldCat.org
- most electronic content products
- discovery services, such as Summon, EBSCO Discovery Service, and Primo Central
- some library automation products:
  - Apollo from Biblionix
  - the 360 suite from ProQuest
  - EBSCO A–Z, LinkSource, etc.
- library services platforms offered as multi-tenant services, including OCLC's WorldShare Management Services or Ex Libris's Alma.

A variety of benefits are gained through multi-tenant applications in the library arena. Vendors that offer a product based on this architecture operate a single instance of the code base that is able to take advantage of a large pool of hardware resources and software components. Adding new customers increases resource consumption by only small increments. Database tunings, configurations, software patches, and other routine system maintenance activities can be done once and applied globally. For companies serving a large customer base, maintaining a single large multi-tenant platform can be accomplished with fewer technical personnel compared to having to install and maintain thousands of separate institutional instances. Patches applied to the software to fix bugs take effect for all customers at once, compared to having to perform upgrades to hundreds or thousands of separate servers.

Applications can evolve gracefully in a multi-tenant environment. New features or fixes to existing functionality can be added to the global instance on a frequent schedule since this model does not impose software installation tasks on end users. Some needed enhancements, such as those needed to address a security issue, may be deployed entirely transparently to end users. Significant changes in the behavior of the system might be offered initially as optional features that can be tested by end users before becoming activated in the production platform.

Libraries benefit from multi-tenant platforms as well. Given that all the technical administration is executed by the vendor, the burden to the library is very light. In most cases the library will not need to allocate technical personnel for the administration related to their use of the system. In larger libraries, there may be higher-level tasks that require the attention of a systems librarian or functional expert related to institutional configuration issues, data loading, or interactions with other local systems. Smaller libraries will operate these products with very little local intervention.

From the library perspective any form of hosting can reduce the need for managing local equipment and its associated involvement of technical personnel. The difference between the vendor hosting a server-oriented system and a multi-tenant platform is more subtle from the library's perspective. Either version shifts responsibility for the technical infrastructure from the local institution to the vendor.

- Multi-tenant systems may offer built-in content resources, such as knowledge bases and bibliographic data sources.
- Multi-tenant systems usually offer a higher-level, more abstract configuration process.
- Server-oriented systems may perform well in implementations with very high transaction loads. The hardware can be scaled and software optimized to handle peak periods. Most large urban libraries, for example, continue to rely on locally hosted server-oriented integrated library systems.

For many libraries the practical differences between a vendor-hosted server-oriented system (ASP) and a multi-tenant platform can be subtle. Whether the technical architecture of a product is multi-tenant or relies on a separate institutional instance may have a relatively small impact on how the software functions for a library. The difference between a system housed and managed by the institution versus either of the hosted models (SaaS or ASP) makes substantial operational impact.

Web-Based Interfaces

Library services platforms provide web-based interfaces, requiring no local software in servers or staff workstations. The integrated library system emerged during the client/server phase of technology. These products were based on data stores and business logic residing on servers housed in the data center of the library and software installed on library staff workstations that provided a graphical user interface that performed some processing, usually related to error checking, communications optimization, and presentation-oriented tasks to off-load processing from the central servers. Library services platforms, in contrast, provide all functionality to library personnel via interfaces presented through their web browsers. The data stores and business logic reside on a multi-tenant platform hosted by the vendor, eliminating the requirement for a local server, or an institutional server hosted by the vendor or other colocation provider. Delivering all interfaces via web browsers eliminates the often substantial overhead involved in the installation and upgrades of staff workstation clients and institutional server software, hardware, and operating systems.

Services-Oriented Architecture

The current preferred framework for software development is based on the creation of high-level functionality composed of many reusable lower-level granules of functionality called services. This services-oriented approach enables efficient and flexible software development since each small task need only be coded once. Low-level services can be organized into middleware that provides a generalized set of resources for higher-level business applications. Domain-specific functionality can be developed on top of the middleware layer to focus development on unique work rather than tasks common to most software applications.

APIs Exposed for Extensibility and Interoperability

In addition to the interfaces provided for staff to use via their web browsers, library services platforms also provide application programming interfaces. These interfaces are not consumed by humans, but rather listen to requests from external systems or programs and provide appropriate responses. APIs can enable advanced reporting capabilities by providing data managed within the system to external applications that will calculate statistics, perform analysis, and control formatting. APIs can also be used to programmatically update data, such as global changes or other tasks that may not be built into the staff interfaces. APIs that perform updates are generally carefully secured and limited to authorized personnel or processes to avoid accidental changes or data corruption. In the same way that all of the functionality of the staff interface must be well documented, the developer of the system must also provide detailed documentation of each of the APIs exposed.

Interoperability

Library services platforms interoperate with external applications such as ERP (enterprise resource planning), financial systems, student account management, and learning management systems via APIs rather than batch loads of records. For many institutions, the library and its resource management systems represent only one component of the technical infrastructure that supports the enterprise. Library systems often consume data managed by another system, such as receiving patron records from a university's student management and human resource management systems. The financial data and transactions managed by the library's acquisitions processes often need to be transmitted into the financial management of its higher-level institution. Ideally, these data transfer and synchronization tasks can be accomplished through the APIs of the respective systems. At a minimum, data files can be extracted via APIs that can then be imported or loaded into an external system.

Subscription Pricing

Providers generally offer library services platforms through a subscription-based business model. For installed software, for large applications such as an integrated library system, the business model was based on an initial amount paid for the initial license, plus additional annual charges for ongoing maintenance and support. Software-as-a-service is usually offered through an annual subscription fee set according to the size and complexity of the organization. The first year might include some additional costs associated with migration and setup. The fixed cost of the subscription displaces a variety of direct and indirect costs associated with installed software applications, including hardware, operating systems, and data center environment, as well as technical personnel. The annual subscription cost for an SaaS product is generally higher than the maintenance fees associated with a locally hosted application, but the total costs should generally be comparable when all expense categories are calculated.

A MATURING SET OF PRODUCTS

Library services platforms can no longer be considered "next-generation systems," but rather by now well-established products that have seen implementations in hundreds of libraries. The conceptual design of the products, which later became known as library services platforms, began in 2009. Multiple organizations entered an intense phase of product development that culminated with some implementations as early as December 2010. By the end of 2015, almost 1,700 libraries had implemented one of the available library services platforms. Many others have signed contracts for a library services platform and are in the installation process.

From Development to Implementation Phase

Library services platforms have been in the deployment phase for several years, providing an increasing body of evidence regarding their efficacy. Information gathered from libraries that gained firsthand experience with these products can boost confidence in whether they perform as advertised or if they fail to fulfill expectations. Such assessment data can apply to a new product genre or concept, to the individual products that constitute that genre, and to a product's use in specific types of libraries.

The maturity of a product can be considered in terms of a series of benchmarks, including the following.

- Completion of initial development. Has the development of the initial version of the product been completed? The initial version may not provide every feature anticipated, but to be considered complete, it should address the full range of functionality at some level.
- Early production phase. At least a small number of libraries have implemented the product and are using it as their daily operational system and have been able to decommission their incumbent systems.
- Mass deployment. The product is considered a routine offering, with dozens or hundreds of libraries using it in production.

Technology products seem to never achieve a final point of development when they might be considered "finished." Even integrated library systems, which have been on the market for decades, continue to see enhancements to provide new features and capabilities, to fix bugs, and to address security issues. New products, such as library services platforms, will usually see intense ongoing development following the initial version. This ongoing development may result in new features, increased stability, or faster performance, which will be deployed incrementally. Products deployed through multi-tenant platforms can be enhanced gradually, rather than in the large-step version releases of the previous generation.

Sources to Assess Implementation Patterns and Acceptance

A variety of resources are available that help libraries assess the maturity of a product in terms of its development cycle and implementation patterns.

"Library Systems Report," published annually by *American Libraries*, includes sales statistics and other data provided by vendors for each of their major products. This report covers integrated library systems, library services platforms, discovery services, and other strategic library products. The number of sales and installations reported provide an important measure of the acceptance and maturity of the product. This report continues the "Automation Marketplace" published in *Library Journal* that I authored between 2002 and 2012.

Implementation data from libraries.org. *Library Technology Guides* includes the libraries.org directory, which documents the strategic automation products used in libraries in addition to other details. The data in libraries.org cannot be considered comprehensive, but it is the most complete resource for this type of data. It provides strong coverage of public and academic libraries in North America and Europe. Particular attention has been given to documenting the libraries that have been involved with selecting and subsequently implementing library services platforms. Statistics and charts from libraries.org are used in this report to illustrate the adoption patterns of library services platforms.

"Library Automation Perceptions Survey." Conducted through *Library Technology Guides*, the "Library Automation Perceptions Survey" has been conducted annually since 2007.

Development Strategies: Greenfield versus Brownfield

How quickly an organization can develop an incredibly complex software application such as a library services platform relates to many factors. Organizations with a large development capacity will have an advantage. The number of personnel allocated for software development provides one metric. Organizations with a development team's programming infrastructure already in place will naturally have an advantage over those that must recruit, train, and establish new processes and procedures. Each of the organizations involved in the development of library services platforms is relatively large, with personnel allocated to product design, software architecture, programming, quality assurance, and testing.

Another interesting aspect of library services platforms concerns the extent to which each is an entirely new product and which have built upon existing components. One can use concepts in the software development realm borrowed from other kinds of projects. Software projects can be considered "greenfield" or "brownfield" depending on whether they incorporate previous development efforts. Definitions of these terms as applied to software development are given in *Wikipedia:*

> "Brownfield development is a term commonly used in the IT industry to describe problem spaces needing the development and deployment of new software systems in the immediate presence of existing (legacy) software applications/systems."[4]

> "A greenfield is a project that lacks any constraints imposed by prior work. The analogy is to that of construction on greenfield land where there is no need to work within the constraints of existing buildings or infrastructure."[5]

In the library services arena, a distinct trade-off can be seen in the greenfield versus brownfield approaches. A brownfield project has the potential to shorten the development phase, but it can also moderate the extent to which the product is able to thoroughly revise functionality and be expressed through new technology architectures and infrastructure components. The offerings in the genre of library services platform exhibit varying development strategies.

OCLC WorldShare Management Services took the greenfield model. An entirely new technology platform was created for the service. It is not known to have borrowed programming code or components from any of the integrated library systems that the company has acquired (Amlib, OLIB, LBS, CBS, Sisis Sunrise, and BOND Bibliotheca). The WorldShare Platform does leverage the content of the massive WorldCat bibliographic service. It also uses the existing OCLC Connexion as its initial cataloging interface as it works toward a full cataloging module based on the WorldShare Platform. OCLC also positions the existing WorldCat Local service as the discovery interface for World-Share Management Services. In 2014 OCLC launched WorldCat Discovery Service on a new platform to eventually replace WorldCat Local and its First-Search service.[6]

The development of Alma by Ex Libris can be seen as a greenfield project. Alma was developed on an entirely new code base apart from its Voyager and Aleph integrated library systems, its Verde electronic resource management system, and its SFX link resolver. The company had two existing integrated library systems that were both quite successful, with ongoing use in some of the world's largest and most prestigious libraries. Voyager was developed by

Endeavor Information Systems, seeing its first production use at Michigan Technological University in December 1995. Aleph, originally developed in the 1980s, had evolved through multiple cycles of technology, but was not considered appropriate as the basis for the company's new strategic platform. The content of the Alma knowledge base incorporated and extended the one created for SFX, but the platform and code are new. Ex Libris packages Primo and Primo Central as the discovery service for Alma. Primo was itself a green-field service, created in 2006, that has been enhanced and extended over its product history.

The Kuali OLE project can be considered a hybrid approach. The code base for the domain-specific functionality of Kuali OLE is entirely new. The project opted to make use of software components, including the Kuali Rice middleware and Kuali Financial System. Kuali Rice provides a modern services-oriented foundation, but it was not created to support multi-tenant services. Kuali Financial System is in the process of being redeveloped by the new KualiCo organization.

Innovative Interfaces was able to leverage a significant portion of the Millennium code base in the development of Sierra. Throughout its corporate history, Innovative has based its development strategy on building on established functionality. In creating Sierra, Innovative preserved the layer of the Millennium code base that supports the business logic and functionality, surrounded by new technology for database management, a layer that exposes the functionality through the services-oriented architecture, and a new set of Java-based staff clients. As can be seen in table 7.1, this brownfield approach enabled the creation of Sierra through a much shorter development phase than those that followed the greenfield model.

SirsiDynix has taken a hybrid approach. Its BLUEcloud suite can be considered a library services platform since it embodies many of the characteristics of the genre. It is deployed through a multi-tenant web-based platform, manages electronic and print resources, and delivers its functionality through browser-based interfaces. At this point in its development, however, the

TABLE 7.1
Development Phase for Library Service Platforms

Product	Announcement	First Production	Time
Alma	July 2009	July 2012	36
WMS	April 2009	Nov 2010	20
Sierra	April 2011	April 2012	12
Kuali OLE	June 2008	Aug 2014	49
Intota	June 2011	—	42 (to date)

BLUEcloud suite relies on the implementation of one of the SirsiDynix integrated library systems, Symphony or Horizon.

The development timeline of the library services platforms reflects, as expected, a longer period of development for the products that are developed through the greenfield model. Ex Libris was able to create the initial version of Alma in around thirty-six months from the time that its intention to develop the product was announced. The initial production of Kuali OLE came just under fifty months following the beginning of its initial planning project, with more time and work underway until the full version that manages electronic resources had been completed and implemented.

Given the uneven state of development, libraries may question whether they should move forward with the consideration of new systems or wait until more systems have become more complete and have seen implementation. One line of reasoning might suggest that a library should wait until all of the products have been completed, reached a certain state of maturity, and seen production implementations. Others might argue that there are at least some products in the genre that are finished, at least in their initial versions, and have seen hundreds of production implementations. Libraries especially interested in open source software may find it worthwhile to wait to observe the progress of Kuali OLE, especially regarding the anticipated capabilities to also manage electronic resources.

The number of offerings in the genre of library services platforms remains relatively narrow. Compared to the number of integrated library systems that have been developed over the history of library automation, this number seems uncomfortably small. We have also seen an often painful process of product consolidation that has taken place through the mergers and acquisitions of the last decade or two. It is not likely that the genre of library services platforms will expand in the near future. Each of the current products is produced by quite strong organizations, providing a reasonable level of confidence that each of these products will endure and reach ever higher levels of maturity and adoption.

LIBRARY SERVICES PLATFORM
OR INTEGRATED LIBRARY SYSTEM

Despite the emergence of the genre of library services platforms, integrated library systems remain a viable option for many libraries. The integrated library system has been the cornerstone of library automation since the mid-1970s and will continue into the future. These two products will continue to coexist for the foreseeable future.

The advent of library services platforms has split the library resource management arena into two threads of development. These two categories cannot, however, be considered as entirely distinct. There are considerable areas of overlap, and some of the directions of development underway in the integrated library system arena may bring these two categories to increasing levels of overlap in the future.

There is already considerable movement among the integrated library systems to shift to all browser-based interfaces, to offer online catalogs with increasing characteristics of discovery interfaces, and to manage multiple types of materials.

Significant development has taken place among the integrated library systems widely used in public libraries to support integrated management and lending of e-books. This integration includes staff-oriented tools to more easily manage the acquisition of new titles from the major e-book providers, but to also conduct the lending and the provision of the e-book to library patrons through the interface of the library's catalog or discovery interface. These advancements have been seen more in the integrated library systems oriented to public libraries, such as Polaris, Library.Solution, and Apollo. E-book integration has been a strategic emphasis of BiblioCommons.

Another configuration takes a hybrid approach to the integrated library system and the library services platform. The SirsiDynix BLUEcloud includes a suite of applications that fall well within the definition of library services platform. Its components including eResource Central, the BookMyne mobile platform, and functional modules such as BLUEcloud Circulation and BLUEcloud Cataloging—all reside on a web-native multi-tenant platform. These products do not operate entirely independently, but rely on an implementation of one of SirsiDynix's integrated library systems, either Symphony or Horizon. SirsiDynix has developed a set of APIs for Symphony and Horizon, called Web Services, that expose the APIs needed to participate in the BLUEcloud environment as well as interoperate with other external scripts or applications.[7]

One sees considerable overlap between the product genres of ILSs and library service platforms. The November 2013 issue of *Smart Libraries Newsletter* addressed some of the considerations that apply between integrated library systems and library services platforms. That article suggested that at least some of the integrated library systems were evolving into a more progressive set of characteristics that embody increasing similarities to library services platforms. Table 7.2 shows an updated version of the matrix of considerations highlighting this evolutionary track of development.

Some degree of affinity can be seen between the type of library and the category of resource management system adopted.

Library services platforms currently see higher levels of adoption by academic libraries than other types. Academic libraries face a major operational challenge in managing collections of predominantly electronic resources with

TABLE 7.2

Matrix of General Features of the Categories of Resource Management Systems

Category	Integrated Library System	Progressive Integrated Library System	Library Services Platform
Resources managed	Physical	print, electronic	electronic, physical
Technology platform	server-based	server-based	multi-tenant SaaS
Knowledge bases	None	none	e-holdings, bibliographic
Patron interfaces	browser-based	browser-based	browser-based
Staff interfaces	graphical desktop (Java Swing, Windows, Mac OS)	browser-based	browser-based
Procurement models	Purchase	purchase, license	license
Hosting option	local install, ASP	local install, ASP	SaaS only
Interoperability	batch transfer, proprietary API	batch transfer, RESTful APIs,	APIs (mostly RESTful)
Products	SirsiDynix Symphony and Horizon, Millennium, Polaris	Sierra, SirsiDynix Symphony/ BLUEcloud, Polaris, Apollo	WorldShare Management Services, Alma, Sierra, Kuali OLE
Development strategy	Brownfield	brownfield	greenfield (mixed)

the ongoing need to maintain their print collections. The fundamental tenet of library services platforms to provide comprehensive resource management spanning content format types directly addresses this need.

Public libraries continue to see vigorous circulation of their physical collections, supplemented by an increasing portion of lending of e-books and other digital materials. Integrated library systems, especially with the e-book lending integration tools now available, continue to serve public libraries well.

School libraries have quite specialized needs, including the need to manage relatively small collections of print books with special attention to selections by reading level. These libraries also offer access to electronic resources, but in somewhat different ways than university and college libraries dealing primarily with issues relating to age-appropriate resources. School libraries primarily make use of specialized integrated library systems and discovery tools from companies such as Follett, Book Systems, Alexandria, and others.

TABLE 7.3

Distribution of Implementations by Library Type

Product	Academic	Public	School	Special	Other	Libraries	Installations
Alma	269	1	0	31	63	364	111
WorldShare	171	9	7	11	26	224	175
Kuali OLE							
Sierra	367	1,134	9	13	101	1,624	452
Intota							

Table 7.3 provides data describing the types of libraries that have implemented each of the products. The counts represent the library organizations that are known to have selected each product as recorded in the libraries .org database. As with other data taken based on libraries.org, caveats apply. Numbers shown were taken at the end of 2014. While this is a group of products very closely tracked, some implementations are not made public, so in some cases numbers may be somewhat lower than total reported by vendors. Library counts represent a very rough measure. Some libraries may include multiple branches or facilities, and there is substantial variation in the collection size and other metrics of each library. These figures show that the number of installations is much larger than the number of libraries represented, illustrating that many have implemented these products via consortial arrangements.

SUPPORT FOR LIBRARY CONSORTIA

From the earliest phase of the history of library automation, organizations have worked together to share systems to lower costs and to expand the pool of resources available to the users. So while sharing systems among the members of a consortium is not new, recent years have seen many new large-scale projects. Notable examples include these:

Illinois Heartland Library System (427 libraries) has consolidated the systems of four previous regional library systems into a single implementation of Polaris.

The *approximately 100 public libraries of Northern Ireland* have implemented SirsiDynix Symphony as they consolidated four previous consortia.

All of the public libraries in the Republic of Ireland announced their selection of Sierra to serve all of the 32 public library services that include around 170 individual branches, consolidating the individual incumbent implementations.

The *public libraries of the state of South Australia* have recently completed the implementation of a statewide automation system using Sirsi-Dynix Symphony, consolidating many previously independent integrated library system implementations.

There have also been some high-profile projects that provide shared technology infrastructure to large groups of academic libraries through shared instances of library services platforms.

The *Orbis Cascade Alliance* completed the implementation of its 37 academic library members on January 7, 2015. These libraries had previously worked together as a consortium to share resources using separate integrated library systems and resource-sharing technology. The consortium originally used Innovative's INN-reach to facilitate resource-sharing requests and routing, changing to WorldCat Navigator in 2008. In October 2012, the Alliance announced its selection of Ex Libris Alma as a single shared automation system for all of its members.

Following a long planning and procurement process, *Wales Higher Education Libraries Forum* (WHELF), a consortium of the national library and the major academic libraries in Wales, announced its selection of Alma as the basis of its shared library management strategy.

All 23 campuses of the University of California which previously had implemented separate integrated library systems have selected Ex Libris Alma as a shared library services platform for the entire CSU system.

The *BIBSYS* consortium of 105 members that includes the National Library of Norway and the major academic and research libraries, selected Ex Libris Alma in December 2013. BIBSYS had previously developed its own system to serve its members.

The *LIBROS* consortium of 16 academic institutions in the state of New Mexico announced its selection of OCLC's WorldShare Management Services in January 2014. By late December 2014, all of the libraries had completed their migrations.

The *Private Academic Library Network of Indiana* (PALNI), a consortium of 23 academic libraries, has implemented WorldShare Management Services.

Cooperating Libraries in Consortium, a consortium of the academic libraries of eight small colleges and universities, has selected ProQuest Intota and has implemented Summon and the foundation release while continuing to operate its Millennium integrated library system.

Other projects known to be investigating or in the procurement process for a shared resource management environment include these:

VALID, a group of academic institutions in the state of New Jersey. Representatives of this group have been involved in the Kuali OLE project, working toward the possibility of a shared consortial implementation. No specific timetable has been announced.

The 40 *publicly funded universities and community colleges in the state of Florida* are in the process of setting a new strategy for a shared automation system. Florida has a history of shared automation systems, with the community colleges and universities each operating statewide systems. Currently the community colleges share a single implementation of Ex Libris Aleph, while each of the universities uses separate instances of Aleph, with a shared discovery interface. Consideration is now underway for a system to be shared among both groups. An "Invitation to Negotiate Next Generation Integrated Library System" was issued on December 15, 2014, by the Complete Florida Plus Program, the organization with a portfolio that includes responsibility for library automation with a contract expected in 2016.[8] (https://libraries.flvc.org/monthly-updates-february-2016).

NOTES

1. Marshall Breeding, "Smarter Libraries through Technology: The Beginning of the End of the ILS in Academic Libraries," *Smart Libraries Newsletter* 31, no. 8 (August 2011): 1–2, http://journals.ala.org/sln/issue/viewIssue/302/64.
2. Marshall Breeding, "A Cloudy Forecast for Libraries," *Computers in Libraries* 31, no. 7 (September 2011): 32–35.
3. Marshall Breeding, "E-resource Knowledge Bases and Link Resolvers: An Assessment of the Current Products and Emerging Trends," *Insights: The UKSG Journal* 25, no. 2 (2012): 173–82.
4. *Wikipedia*, s.v. "Brownfield (Software Development)," last modified December 2, 2014, http://en.wikipedia.org/wiki/Brownfield_%28software_development%29.
5. *Wikipedia*, s.v. "Greenfield Project," last modified January 3, 2015, http://en.wikipedia.org/wiki/Greenfield_project.
6. See Marshall Breeding, "OCLC Announces WorldCat Discovery Service," *Smart Libraries Newsletter* 34, no. 3 (2014): 6–7, http://journals.ala.org/sln/issue/view/271.

7. Marshall Breeding, "Smarter Libraries through Technology: The Roles of Integrated Library Systems and Library Services Platforms," *Smart Libraries Newsletter* 33, no. 3 (2013): 1–4, http://journals.ala.org/sln/issue/view/283.
8. See http://uwf.edu/media/university-of-west-florida/offices/procurement/bids/14itn-04aj/14ITN-04AJ.pdf.

8
Criteria for Purchasing
E-book Platforms

There is no one-size-fits-all model when deciding which platforms to choose for the delivery of e-books. Every library's needs are different, and no two products provide the same features and functionalities—even when catering to the same type of library audience. Librarians usually start to get acquainted with a platform (or vendor) by asking questions about the content available and compatibility to make sure that they have the equipment in place to support the product. Then they move on to questions about the terms of the licensing agreement and a host of other topics that usually have to do with one of the following areas: content, technical specifications, functionality, and business model.

Mirela Roncevic is a content developer, editor, writer, and advocate for editors and writers. She has written and edited countless articles, features, book reviews, and newsletters; set editorial direction for books and book series; and developed content for publishing and library professionals.

CONTENT

Questions pertaining to content can usually be answered by simply browsing each product's website. Publishers and vendors tend to be forthright about the scope of their platforms. It is important to get a good sense of how big these platforms are to understand the logic behind their complex pricing structures. And these platforms run the gamut: from those hosting hundreds of thousands of e-books to those hosting a few hundred titles by one or two publishers. With most business models, a general rule applies: the greater the scope, the greater the value; the greater the value, the higher the price.

The following content-specific questions usually arise in discussions with library vendors: How many books are included overall? Do I need to purchase all of them? What library markets is the platform built for? Who is the primary audience? What types of e-books are available on the platform (e.g., reference books, trade titles from major houses, monographs)? In the case of subject-specific or publisher-specific e-book platforms, what are the key subjects covered? And how often are new titles added to the platform?

When examining aggregator and distributor platforms, librarians want to know about the overall number of publishers represented to determine how many of those publishers' titles they can expect to circulate in the library. Keeping up with titles and publishers is no small task, since most e-book platforms are updated on a monthly, and some on a weekly, basis. Major aggregators are constantly signing new deals and announcing new partnerships with publishers to boost their offerings.

For research and learning purposes, librarians will want to know about the inclusion of multimedia in the package. Are there videos, images, and other tools that help enhance the reading experience? What about integration of other types of content? What else is included in the package other than e-books? Journals? Databases? Lastly, is there a sister product associated with the platform that librarians should be aware of?

Here is an outline of the various content factors to consider when choosing e-book platforms:

- type of e-book platform (e.g., by publisher, aggregator, wholesaler, university press, e-book lending service)
- primary library market (e.g., public, K–12, academic, corporate, government)
- number of titles
- number of publishers and/or imprints
- types of e-books on the platform (e.g., trade books, reference books, monographs, K–12 nonfiction)
- expected growth/frequency of updates (how often new titles are added)

- subjects covered (e.g., fiction, general nonfiction, arts and humanities, science and technology)
- inclusion of multimedia (e.g., images, videos, interactive maps)
- integration of content other than e-books (e.g., journals)
- inclusion of book reviews
- inclusion of author biographies and other works by the same author
- distributor partner (e.g., Yankee Book Peddler)
- offspring (related products)

TECHNICAL SPECIFICATIONS

Technical specs involve discussions about the equipment needed for the library or user to access e-books, browsers supported, software or plug-ins needed, file formats of e-books, and compatible e-readers. Most e-book platforms support all browsers, including Google Chrome, Internet Explorer, Safari, and Firefox. Librarians need to keep in mind that not all patrons own portable reading devices and may still be reading e-books on their home computers. Knowing in advance which browsers the platform supports and whether any additional software installations are needed (e.g., Adobe Digital Editions) will determine if the e-book platform reflects the needs of their community.

E-books are generally licensed (or less commonly sold) to libraries in PDF and ePub file formats. These two formats are supported by the majority of reading devices, including Nook, iPad, Sony eReader, and Kobo. Kindle uses its own proprietary format known as AZW. ePub is considered to be the industry standard preferred by librarians. Most vendors whose platforms support only PDF are working toward making their e-books available in ePub. Librarians usually recommend buying e-books in ePub, XHTML, or other XML-based formats because the files are reflowable and can better adapt their presentation to the output device. PDF files generally do not adapt as well to mobile devices and are difficult to view on small screens. If PDF is the only file format offered by the vendor, text-based Adobe PDF formats are a good alternative because they support highlighting, keyword searching, and disability access.

Clearly, not all e-books may be read on all devices. This is one of the most challenging aspects of how e-books have evolved in recent years. While the number of dedicated e-readers continues to grow, so does the frustration surrounding the limitations imposed on users who own only one reading device or a library able to afford only one type of e-book platform. The most prevalent portable e-readers include Barnes & Noble's Nook, Apple's iPad, Sony's eReader, Kobo, and Amazon's Kindle. The Kindle is widely considered to be the most user-friendly e-book reading device since it uses the patron's Amazon account as the delivery source for content.

Here is an outline of the technical factors to consider when choosing e-book platforms:

- browsers supported (e.g., Internet Explorer, Safari, Firefox, Google Chrome)
- software requirements (e.g., Adobe Digital Editions)
- plug-in requirements
- file formats (e.g., ePub, PDF, HTML)
- availability of an app
- hand-held e-readers supported (e.g., Nook, iPad, Kindle, Kobo, Sony eReader)
- availability of a proprietary reader by the vendor
- compatibility with ILS (integrated library system)
- integration with the library's OPAC

FUNCTIONALITY

Functionality is all about the bells and whistles associated with each platform. Librarians need to be aware of the different features available and how valuable they may be both to the library (e.g., COUNTER reports) and to the patrons (e.g., ability to print). Academic librarians will be most interested in the embedded tools that support research, including full-text searching at book and chapter level, annotation and citation tools, persistent URLs, generous copy/paste and printing options, and content availability for offline reading.

The availability of usage data (e.g., COUNTER), ADA-compliant features, and MARC records are of interest to all libraries. E-book catalogs can range from having MARC records available for every e-book title offered by the library to not having any. The majority of vendors, especially those with a large number of reference books, provide MARC records.

Here is an outline of the various functionality factors to consider when choosing e-book platforms:

- full-text searching
- keyword searching
- copy/paste options
- printing options
- downloading options
- searching at article, book, and collection level
- advanced search capabilities (truncation, Boolean)
- bookmarking within e-books
- citation tools

- annotation tools
- offline reading
- availability of usage reports
- persistent URLs (book, chapter, collection level)
- print-on-demand copy service
- ADA compliance
- personalization features
- availability of MARC records

BUSINESS MODELS

Dealing with business models and understanding the multitude of pricing options available is the most complicated—and controversial—part of e-book acquisition. It requires constantly keeping up with various policies and business practices, which change continually owing to the mergers that occur within the industry and to the technological advances that make it possible for companies to upgrade purchasing plans more frequently. Many questions need to be answered before a library can sign a contract with a vendor and commit to an e-book platform. Since pricing options are usually not explained at length on vendor sites, librarians need to take a proactive approach and explore all viable alternatives.

Here is a sampling of typical business model questions a vendor sales representative may encounter: Is this a subscription platform or purchase-to-own business model? If I choose to purchase e-books to own, are there annual access fees associated with using the platform? Can they be waived if a certain number of e-books are purchased in advance? If I opt for a subscription package, what happens to the content after my contract expires? How frequently will my library be invoiced? Can I view the product before purchasing (and without needing to sign up for an institutional trial)? What DRM policies should I be aware of? And what about embargoes? How long will my library need to wait before it can offer best-selling titles? Although publishers don't wait as long as they used to to release e-versions of print titles, some still impose an embargo period before e-book versions are available for library lending.

Since many e-book vendors charge the cost of a print title plus a certain percentage for their e-books, librarians want to know what the cost of each title is in relation to its print counterpart. They also want to know about single versus multiple versus unlimited use of each e-book. Some platforms allow for an unlimited use of their e-books (by any number of readers at any time), while others adhere to a one title/one user model. Some offer unlimited access for older titles but impose a one title/one user model for new releases. Access policies vary widely among vendors, and they are not always set in stone. If a vendor has only one business model in place at launch, it is not unusual for the vendor to revise its policy in six months to offer more options.

Demand-driven acquisition (DDA), also referred to as patron-driven acquisition, is one of the most talked-about models for acquiring e-books in academic libraries. Offered by both publishers and aggregators, the PDA model is fairly straightforward: e-book purchases are triggered based on traffic and patron interest in particular titles. In other words, patrons' use of a book triggers purchase. (Various trigger and price points are offered.) This business model guarantees that only the content that gets used gets purchased. Although DDA is not as common in public libraries, some libraries and vendors are experimenting with it.

Short-term loans (STL) may be a good solution for librarians looking to obtain access to content they wouldn't be able to afford to buy. STLs are similar to the DDA model in that patron demand ultimately drives what the library budget is spent on. The key difference is that STLs are about renting e-books instead of buying them. Patrons borrow titles directly from the aggregator's catalog (not owned by the library) and get access to a title for a set period of time (usually one, two, three, seven, fourteen, or thirty days) and the library is charged for the rental. This costs the library anywhere from 5 to 30 percent of the title price. (Loan prices escalate according to the number of days required for the loan.)

One popular way to save money when purchasing e-books is via library consortia. Many vendors have arrangements with consortia that provide e-books to libraries at discounted rates. As is the case with other alternatives, librarians will encounter both benefits and drawbacks when choosing the consortial route. Benefits include more e-books for less money and equality of content across libraries; minimal energy spent on licensing agreements; and e-book lending across a wide variety of libraries. There are also challenges to note. Since publishers don't benefit as much when libraries share access, they often put pressure on aggregators to limit the size of consortia. In addition, certain member libraries may have unique needs that are not in line with those of other members, or they may not want to spend money on titles that others want to buy. On the public library side, larger consortia mean longer queues of popular trade titles.

Here is an outline of the business model factors to consider when choosing e-book platforms:

- one user/one book model
- purchase-to-own option
- subscription option
- short-term loans
- demand-driven acquisition (DDA)

- free viewing period (for DDA)
- perpetual archive fee
- title cost relative to print cost
- minimum commitment
- interlibrary loan (ILL)
- invoicing intervals (monthly, quarterly, yearly)
- DRM policies
- use of content via classroom projection devices (e.g., interactive whiteboards)
- annual maintenance fee
- free trials (length)
- pay-per-view option
- availability of pre-built subject collections
- consortial purchasing
- approval plans
- embargo period

Index